RAY HINISH

One Insight Away

How One Insight Can Free You from Stress, Struggle, and Self-Doubt Forever

First edition

This book was professionally typeset on Reedsy.
Find out more at reedsy.com

To my loving and supportive wife, Sheri and my amazing children: Shea, Ray, and Ary. I wake up every morning in blissful gratitude that I am lucky enough to have you all in my life.

Contents

Introduction

"Thought is not reality; yet it is through thought that our realities are created." — Sydney Banks

What if everything you've been told about changing your life is wrong? Right now, as you read these words, you're probably carrying something heavy. Maybe it's anxiety that follows you like a shadow, whispering worst-case scenarios about your future. Maybe it's the weight of past mistakes that replay in your mind like a broken record. Maybe it's the exhausting effort of trying to manage your thoughts, control your emotions, and fix everything that feels wrong with your life.

You've likely tried the conventional approaches: therapy to process your past, meditation to quiet your mind, positive thinking to reprogram your beliefs, goal-setting to create your future. Some of these may have helped temporarily, but here you are, still searching, still struggling, still feeling like something fundamental is missing.

What if I told you that the very premise underlying all of these approaches— that you need to work hard to change your life—is based on a misunderstanding so profound that once you see through it, everything shifts?

What if the transformation you've been seeking isn't months or years away, but literally one insight away?

The Moment Everything Changed

Two years ago, I was sitting in a retreat center in Jamaica, holding eight capsules of psychedelic mushrooms in my palm. I wasn't there because I was particularly spiritual—I was there because I was drowning in my own desires for success and accomplishment. Despite a life that appeared successful on the outside, I was drowning in my own thinking, caught in endless loops of anxiety, self-doubt, and the exhausting effort of trying to manage my mental state.

The problem was, my anxiety didn't feel like anxiety. If someone had asked me "Are you anxious?" I would have passed a lie detector test when answering "No." But there are many flavors of anxiety, and my flavor was constant striving, constant achievement, and constant learning. You would have looked at me and seen a guy who loves to learn, someone who reads voraciously and is always working on the next project. But looking back on that time, underneath the surface was an anxiety fueled by the relentless thought "I'm not good enough."

For decades, I had been what you might call a "professional self-improver." I'd read hundreds of books, attended countless seminars, tried every technique and system promising to help me think better, feel better, be better. And while some of these approaches provided temporary relief, none addressed the fundamental problem: I was at war with my own mind.

Then, in one profound moment during that retreat, I heard a voice—whether divine, my own deeper wisdom, or something else entirely—that said simply: "No. You can go. It's that simple."

In that instant, I understood something that had been invisible to me my entire life: all the suffering I thought was so real, so permanent, so much a part of who I was—it was all just thought. And thought, I suddenly saw with crystal clarity, could simply be released.

This wasn't positive thinking or cognitive restructuring. This was seeing through the entire illusion that thoughts are solid, permanent, or meaningful in the way I had always believed them to be.

The Hidden Truth That Changes Everything

What I discovered that day—and what this book will reveal to you—is what I call the Thought Principle. It's based on a profound understanding first articulated by Sydney Banks, a Scottish welder who in 1973 had a spiritual awakening that revolutionized how we understand the human mind.

Here's the truth that can transform your life in an instant: **You are not your thoughts, and the only reason you suffer is because you believe your thoughts to be true.**

This might sound like spiritual philosophy, but it's actually the most practical understanding you could ever have. Because when you really see this—when you feel it in your bones rather than just understand it intellectually—everything changes.

You stop being a victim of your thinking and start recognizing yourself as the space in which all thinking occurs. You stop trying to manage your thoughts and start seeing them for what they really are: temporary mental events with no more substance than clouds passing through the sky.

Why This Understanding Is Different

Unlike every other approach to mental well-being, the Thought Principle doesn't ask you to:

- Analyze your past to understand your patterns
- Practice techniques to manage your emotions
- Work on yourself to become a better person
- Think positively to feel better
- Meditate for years to quiet your mind

Instead, it reveals something that's already true: you are already whole, already wise, already free. You've just been temporarily confused about who you really are and what your thoughts really mean.

This isn't another self-help system that requires discipline and effort. It's a

3

recognition of what's always been available to you—a peace that doesn't depend on circumstances, a clarity that doesn't require thinking, and a freedom that can't be earned because it's what you are.

What You'll Discover in This Book

In the pages that follow, you'll discover why you've been struggling—and how to stop.

You'll finally understand why nothing has worked. Why years of therapy, meditation, positive thinking, and self-help haven't given you the lasting peace you're seeking. It's not because you're broken or doing it wrong—it's because you've been trying to solve the wrong problem.

You'll discover the real source of your suffering. It's not your circumstances, your past, your relationships, or your brain chemistry. It's something far simpler—and far more hopeful—than you've been led to believe.

You'll learn why you feel anxious, depressed, or stuck. And more importantly, you'll see that these states aren't permanent features of who you are—they're temporary experiences created by something you can learn to see through.

You'll understand why your mind feels like your enemy. Why it seems to work against you, creating problems that don't exist and suffering that feels so real. And you'll discover that your mind isn't broken—you've just been misunderstanding how it works.

You'll see through the illusion that's been controlling your life. The belief that your happiness depends on external circumstances, that you need to fix yourself before you can feel good, that peace is something you have to earn or achieve.

You'll experience what it feels like to be free from your own thinking. Not by controlling your thoughts or replacing them with better ones, but by recognizing what you actually are underneath all the mental noise.

You'll discover that you're already amazing. That you don't need to become someone else, heal everything from your past, or perfect your circumstances to experience the peace and happiness you've been seeking.

You'll learn to live with an unshakeable inner calm. I'm not kidding, I really mean unshakeable. Not because your life becomes perfect, but because you'll understand that your well-being was never dependent on life being perfect.

You'll stop being at war with yourself. The exhausting battle with your thoughts, emotions, and circumstances will end—not because you've won the war, but because you'll see there was never a war to fight.

You'll wake up to who you really are. Beneath the anxiety, beneath the self-doubt, beneath all the stories you've believed about yourself, you'll rediscover the peaceful, wise, naturally happy being you've always been.

This isn't another system to learn or technique to practice. This is the end of needing systems and techniques. This is coming home to yourself.

Who This Book Is For

This book is for you if:

- You're tired of being at war with your own mind
- You've tried multiple approaches to feeling better but still struggle
- You sense there's something deeper available than managing your thoughts
- You're ready to discover who you really are beneath all the mental noise
- You want transformation that doesn't require years of work

- You're done with a "white-knuckling approach" to life

This book is especially for those who intuitively know that a 28-point self-help plan or elaborate system will not bring peace and happiness. It's for those who realize there must be a simpler approach to life—one that doesn't require years or decades of study to reap the rewards.

If you're tired of complex frameworks and endless techniques, if you sense that true transformation should be more accessible than the personal development industry suggests, then this book is for you. It's for those who want to skip the line and get straight to the essence of what actually creates lasting change.

This book will show you how to live in a world that seems to conspire to bring you peace and contentment—not because your circumstances become perfect, but because you discover the part of you that was never disturbed by circumstances in the first place.

The transformation you're seeking isn't complex. It doesn't require years of work or perfect implementation of systems. It's available right now, in this moment, through a simple shift in understanding that changes everything.

A Promise and an Invitation

I can't promise that reading this book will solve all your problems or eliminate difficult emotions from your life. What I can promise is that it will show you something about the nature of problems and emotions that might change everything about how you relate to them.

You might discover that most of what you've been trying to fix was never actually broken. You might find that the peace you've been seeking has been here all along. You might realize that you are far more resilient, wise, and capable than you ever imagined.

Most importantly, you might remember something you knew as a child but forgot along the way: life doesn't have to be as heavy or as serious as your thinking makes it seem.

The Journey Begins Now

The understanding you're about to explore isn't mine—it belongs to all of us. It's been discovered and rediscovered throughout history by people who have seen through the illusion of mental suffering to the truth that lies beneath.

You're not reading this book by accident. Something in you knows there's more to life than the mental struggle you've been experiencing. Something in you is ready to come home to who you really are.

That something is your true nature calling you back to itself. And it's been waiting patiently for this moment when you're ready to listen.

The transformation you've been seeking isn't in the future—it's one thought away. The peace you've been chasing isn't somewhere else—it's what you are when you stop chasing.

Welcome to the journey. Welcome home.

1

What Is Thought, Really? (and Why The Thought Principle Will Change Your Life - Forever)

"You're not broken. You're just thinking."

There I am, eight capsules of psychedelic mushrooms resting in my palm like tiny keys to some mysterious door. I glance around at the other participants in our circle—nine strangers, each one nervously eyeing the others as we prepare to dive headfirst into the uncharted waters of our own minds.

A few months earlier, I'd stumbled across a video of a psychedelic researcher from Johns Hopkins University discussing the transformative power of these little fungi. Honestly, it was just background noise while I folded laundry— interesting enough, but nothing that grabbed me by the collar. Until he said something that made me stop mid-fold and rewind the video.

"There was the Beatles before psychedelics," he said, his tone carrying the weight of revelation, "and the Beatles after psychedelics."

The implication hung in the air like incense: these substances had somehow unlocked the potential of a scrappy band of musicians from Liverpool and transformed them into one of the most influential groups in history.

I thought, "I want to know what Ray looks like after psychedelics."

So there I was, months later, at the MycoMeditations retreat center in Jamaica. Ten strangers about to ingest a mind-altering substance for the first time in our lives, surrounded by the kind of ocean scenery that makes you believe in magic even before you've taken anything.

We swallowed our pills and walked to our designated spots. I settled into my chair, put on my blackout eye mask, slipped on noise-canceling headphones with gentle instrumental music, and waited to see where this medicine would take me.

As I sat there, heart hammering against my ribs, I mentally reviewed all the conversations I'd had with friends who'd been on these journeys. They all said the same thing: "It's hard, man. Be prepared to go into the dark corners of your mind and sit in that discomfort. That's where the growth happens—in the darkness."

So I'm sitting there, braced for impact, waiting for the darkness to come. Even though I had no major life trauma to speak of—at forty-eight, my biggest complaint was what you might generously call a mild-to-moderate midlife crisis. Still, I sat ready, chanting in my head: Take me to the darkness.

Then, suddenly, I felt this heat blooming in my chest. I looked down—even though I was wearing a blackout mask—and somehow I could see a darkness in the center of my chest where the burning sensation pulsed. I thought, Okay, here we go, take me to the darkness...

But then, clear as day, I heard a gentle voice in my ears: "No. You can go. It's that simple."

In that instant, I watched the darkness dart away like smoke scattered by a strong breeze. The heat vanished, and I had this immediate, unshakable knowing that I was in the presence of something vast and loving and utterly familiar.

For the next six hours, I conversed with this presence—this God, this universal intelligence, whatever you want to call it—like we were old friends catching up over coffee. We bantered, we laughed, and sometimes this presence would teach me something profound with the casual ease of someone pointing out an interesting cloud formation.

At one point, this loving intelligence explained that simple statement: "No. You can go. It's that simple."

The meaning unfolded like origami in reverse: Everything you think is wrong with your life is just thought. Past traumas, current problems, future worries, crushing anxieties—it's all thought. Not even a mental or spiritual scar, really. More like smoke from an extinguished fire, already breaking apart in the breeze.

"No" means you don't have to engage with the thought. "You can go" means the work of that memory, that worry, that fear is done—you've extracted whatever gold there was to find, and there's no reason for the trauma or anxiety to stick around. The thought can simply... leave. "It's that simple" means there's nothing more to do. No need to psychoanalyze it, no need to understand its origins or meaning, no need to fight it. Just let it flow by like a leaf on a river.

The Invisible Power Behind Everything

Most people think of "thought" as just the stuff that happens in your head. Random ideas bouncing around like pinballs. That endless inner narrator who won't shut up at 3 AM, cataloging every mistake you've ever made and every possible disaster that might unfold tomorrow. The mental to-do lists, the judgments, the opinions, the constant commentary on everything and everyone.

But what if I told you that's not really what thought is at all?

What if I told you we've been looking at this whole thing backwards?

We're going to explore something far more foundational than mental chatter. We're going to explore thought—not as noise, but as the invisible power behind every single thing you feel, set, and experience in life.

And here's why this matters: if you misunderstand what thought really is, you'll spend your entire life trying to fix the wrong things.

I spent years doing exactly that. Trying to manage my thoughts like a traffic cop directing rush hour. Attempting to think more positively, as if I could just reprogram my brain like updating software. Reading self-help books that promised I could control my mind if I just tried hard enough, meditated long enough, journaled consistently enough.

But here's what nobody told me: thought is not what you think.

Let me say that again, because it's important. Thought is not what you think.

The Paintbrush and the Canvas

Thought is not just opinions, judgments, beliefs, or ideas. It's not the to-do list running in your head or the voice that analyzes every conversation you had three hours after it's over. It's not even your "inner dialogue"—that running commentary that seems to have opinions about everything from the weather to your life choices.

Those are the products of thought, you could say they are made of thought—like a sculpture is made of clay. But the power behind all that activity? That's the Principle of Thought.

Think of it like this: thought is the paintbrush. Your consciousness (awareness) is the canvas. And your life—everything you experience, every feeling you have, every reality you inhabit—is the painting.

You're not just thinking about life. You're actually feeling thought as reality.

This hit me like a lightning bolt one Tuesday morning. I was standing in my kitchen, coffee mug in hand, spiraling into anxiety about a tough conversation I'd have to have with someone at work. My heart was racing, my palms were sweating, and I was mentally rehearsing all the ways I might completely botch the conversation—how I'd stumble over my words, how they'd get defensive, how the whole thing would blow up in my face and make everything worse.

But then something shifted. For just a moment, I saw it clearly: I wasn't experiencing the conversation. The conversation was still hours away. I was experiencing my thinking about the conversation. The anxiety wasn't coming from some future event—it was coming from the thoughts I was having right now, in my kitchen, with my coffee getting cold.

The conversation itself hadn't happened yet. It might go completely differently than my mental rehearsal. Hell, it might not even happen at all. But there I was, heart pounding, palms sweating, completely consumed by a reality that existed only in my imagination.

Everything Is Thought

Here's what's wild about this: everything you've ever experienced has come through the power of thought.

That heartbreak in high school when Sarah Mitchell told you she just wanted to be friends? Thought.

That feeling of pure awe watching your child sleep, their tiny chest rising and falling in perfect rhythm? Thought.

That anxiety before the big meeting, the job interview, the difficult conversation? Thought.

Even your opinions about what you're reading right now—yep, also thought.

But here's where it gets interesting. We usually think we're experiencing the world. The situation. The past that haunts us. The future that terrifies us. Other people and their moods and their judgments.

But the truth is—you are always and only experiencing your own thinking.

Let me put it another way: You're not living in the feeling of your circumstances. You're living in the feeling of your thinking about your circumstances. No exception.

This isn't just semantics or philosophical word-play. This is the key to peace, clarity, and freedom.

The Dream That Feels Real

Here's the kicker, though: thought doesn't feel like thought. It feels like reality.

When you have the thought, "They don't respect me," you don't experience it as a sentence floating around in your head. You experience it as anger, as tension in your shoulders, as that familiar knot in your stomach. You experience it as defensiveness, as the urge to prove yourself or withdraw completely.

Because consciousness lights thought up. Just like a projector lights up a film on the screen, consciousness makes thought appear real, solid, undeniable.

It's a dreaming-while-awake situation.

Have you ever woken up from a nightmare sweating and panicked? Your heart pounding, your body flooded with adrenaline, even though you were just lying in bed the whole time? That's a thought-created reality. Your mind conjured up an entire experience—complete with emotions, physical sensations, and what felt like life-or-death urgency—out of pure imagination.

And that's your mind... all day long.

The only difference is: when we're awake, we don't realize we're dreaming.

Stepping Out of the Prison

When you start to see that thought is creating your experience moment to moment, something remarkable happens.

You stop blaming.

You stop blaming the past for your current pain. You stop blaming your partner for your frustration. You stop blaming the government, your parents, your circumstances, your genetics, your childhood, your bank account.

You stop blaming yourself.

You realize: "Oh... I'm not broken. I'm just caught in a temporary storm of thought."

That insight alone is like stepping out of a prison you didn't know you were in.

Just like that voice told me in Jamaica: "No. You can go. It's that simple." The darkness I thought I needed to wrestle with, the problems I thought defined me, the anxieties I thought were permanent fixtures of my personality—they were all just smoke from fires that had already been extinguished. They could simply... go.

The Beginning of Freedom

What happens when you start seeing thought as just... thought?

You stop taking every thought so seriously.

You stop needing to fix your feelings, because you realize they're not actually broken—they're just reflecting on whatever's happening in your thinking right now.

You stop over-analyzing everything, because you understand that most of what you're analyzing isn't even real—it's just mental movies playing in the theater of your mind.

And slowly, gradually, like dawn breaking after the longest night, you start to feel lighter.

You realize: "I'm not anxious. I'm just having anxious thoughts."

"I'm not failing. I'm just caught in insecure thinking."

"I'm not stuck. My mind is just spinning—and it will settle."

This isn't positive thinking. This isn't about replacing "bad" thoughts with "good" ones or trying to control what shows up in your mental space.

This is waking up to the nature of experience itself.

The Simple Pause

So here's what I want to leave you with—not as homework or another thing to add to your self-improvement to-do list, but as a gentle invitation.

This week, don't try to manage your thoughts. Don't try to fix them or improve them or make them more positive.

Just notice that they're creating your entire experience.

Start to watch them like clouds passing in the sky. Some are dark and stormy, some are light and fluffy, but they're all temporary. They all pass.

And once a day—maybe when you're brushing your teeth, or waiting for your coffee to brew, or stuck in traffic—ask yourself this simple question:

"What if this isn't the truth? What if it's just a thought?"

That simple pause creates space. And in that space, something beautiful happens.

14

Truth has room to show up.

Not the truth according to your thinking, but the deeper truth that exists underneath all the mental noise. The truth that you are whole, that you are okay, that you are far more resilient and capable and loved than your thoughts would have you believe.

You're not broken. You're just thinking.

And that, my friend, changes everything.

* * *

Key Insights:

- **You're not broken—you're just thinking.** What feels like dysfunction is often just misunderstood thought.
- **Everything you feel is the result of thought.** Not your circumstances, not your past, not other people—but the thoughts passing through your mind right now.
- **Insight is immediate and transformative.** A single insight—like "No, you can go. It's that simple."—can dissolve years of psychological baggage.
- **Thought is not what you think.** It's not just inner chatter, ideas, beliefs, or judgments—it's the *principle* that generates your entire experience.
- **Thought is the paintbrush; consciousness is the canvas; your life is the painting.** What you feel as "reality" is a painting made of thought, lit up by your awareness.
- **You don't experience the world—you experience your thinking about the world.** Your emotional responses arise from perception, not circumstance.
- **Thought feels real because of consciousness.** Like a dream that seems vivid while you're in it, thoughts are animated by awareness and feel true—even when they're not.
- **You can let thought pass without analysis or control.** You don't have to fix, suppress, or change your thoughts—just see them for what they are:

15

passing weather, not permanent truth.

· **Freedom begins with seeing that you live in the feeling of thought.** This realization loosens the grip of fear, anxiety, and insecurity.

· **Ask yourself: "What if this is just a thought?"** This simple pause creates space for truth, presence, and peace to enter.

2

The Story of the Three Principles

"Mental health lies within the consciousness of all human beings, but it is shrouded and held prisoner by our own erroneous thoughts." — *Sydney Banks*

While this book is focused specifically on the Thought Principle, it's important to understand that this principle is one of three fundamental principles discovered by Sydney Banks—a Scottish welder who, in 1973, had a profound spiritual a wakening that would eventually touch the lives of millions of people around the world.

The Three Principles—Mind, Consciousness, and Thought—work together to create all human psychological experience. They are not techniques or methods, but rather the underlying spiritual (or psychological, if you prefer) facts that explain how life works from the inside-out.

The Unlikely Mystic

Sydney Banks was not a spiritual teacher, philosopher, or academic. He was a working-class man living on Salt Spring Island in British Columbia, Canada, with his wife Barb and their children. By his own account, he was an ordinary person dealing with ordinary problems—including severe anxiety, insecurity, and what he later described as a general dissatisfaction with life.

At age 40, Sydney was struggling. He felt insecure about himself, worried constantly about the future, and often felt overwhelmed by life's challenges. He was, by all appearances, just another person trying to make sense of an often confusing and stressful world.

In March of 1973, Sydney and Barb attended a weekend marriage encounter retreat on Cortes Island. The retreat was designed to help couples improve their relationships through various exercises and discussions. Sydney went reluctantly, not expecting much from the experience.

During one of the sessions, a psychologist named Dr. Roger Mills was facilitating a discussion about relationships and personal growth. As the conversation unfolded, Dr. Mills made what seemed like an offhand comment to Sydney: "You're not really insecure, Syd. You just think you are."

For most people, this might have been received as a nice sentiment or perhaps dismissed entirely. But something about those words struck Sydney in a way that defied explanation. In that moment, he experienced what he later called "an explosion of consciousness"—a profound spiritual awakening that completely transformed his understanding of life.

The Awakening

What Sydney experienced in that moment was not just an intellectual insight, but a direct, experiential understanding of the nature of reality itself. He saw, with absolute clarity, that his entire experience of insecurity, anxiety, and personal suffering was being created by his own thinking—not by his circumstances, his past, or any external conditions.

But the realization went far deeper than personal healing. Sydney began to see the fundamental principles behind all human experience. He understood that there were spiritual laws governing psychological life, just as there are physical laws governing the material world.

Over the following days and weeks, Sydney's understanding continued to deepen. He saw that all human beings live in a thought-created reality, that consciousness is what brings thought to life, and that there is a universal intelligence—Mind—that is the source of all mental activity.

The transformation was immediate and permanent. The anxiety and insecurity that had plagued Sydney for decades simply disappeared—not because he had learned to manage them, but because he saw through the illusion that had been creating them.

The Three Principles Revealed

As Sydney's understanding stabilized, he began to articulate what he had seen in terms of three fundamental principles:

Mind is the universal intelligence and life force behind all things. It is the source of all thought and the energy that animates all life. Mind is what allows an acorn to become an oak tree, what keeps the planets in orbit, and what beats your heart without your conscious direction.

Consciousness is the gift of awareness that allows us to experience life. It is what brings thought to life and makes all experience possible. Without consciousness, we would have no awareness of our existence, our thoughts, or our world.

Thought is the creative principle that allows us to experience life through our thinking. All human experience is created through thought, brought to life by consciousness, and powered by the energy of Mind.

These three principles work together seamlessly to create every moment of human experience. They are not separate forces but different aspects of one unified system—like three sides of the same coin.

The Practical Wisdom

Sydney often taught that while understanding all three principles was valuable, people didn't need to worry about all of them equally. As he would explain to audiences:

> "You don't need to worry about Consciousness because you are aware—
> the very fact that you're listening to me right now proves you have

consciousness. You don't need to worry about Mind because it functions beneath the surface, powering and managing everything in existence without your help. Your heart beats, your body heals, the planets stay in orbit—Mind takes care of all of that. The only principle you really need to focus on is Thought, because that's where you have the most interference. That's where you get caught up, where you create your suffering, and where you can find your freedom."

But Sydney was always careful to point out that while thought might be the most practical principle to understand, all three principles are actually the same thing—different aspects of one divine trinity. "You cannot have existence without all three," he would say. "They are one energy, one force, appearing to us as three different aspects so we can understand how life works."

This understanding helped people focus their attention where it would be most helpful while recognizing that they were touching something much larger—the very fabric of existence itself.

Sharing the Understanding

Initially, Sydney had no intention of becoming a teacher. The understanding he had received felt too profound, too simple, and too personal to share. But as friends and neighbors began to notice the dramatic change in him—his peace, his wisdom, his obvious well-being—they started asking questions.

Sydney began sharing what he had seen, not as a teacher or guru, but simply as someone who had discovered something remarkable about the nature of life. He spoke in simple, direct language about the principles he had come to understand, always pointing people toward their own inner wisdom rather than asking them to believe anything he said.

Word of Sydney's understanding began to spread. Mental health professionals, educators, and people from all walks of life came to hear him speak. What they found was not a complex psychological theory or spiritual practice, but a simple, elegant explanation of how the mind works that had immediate practical applications.

The Ripple Effect

Over the following decades, the Three Principles understanding spread around the world. Mental health professionals began incorporating these principles into their work, finding that clients could experience profound healing without years of therapy or analysis. Educators discovered that understanding these principles could transform classroom environments and help students learn more effectively. Business leaders found that this understanding could create more harmonious and productive workplaces.

The principles have been applied in settings ranging from maximum-security prisons to Fortune 500 companies, from inner-city schools to addiction treatment centers. In every case, the results have been the same: when people understand how their experience is actually created, they naturally find their way back to their innate mental health and wisdom.

The Simplicity of Truth

What made Sydney's teaching so powerful was its simplicity. He didn't offer complex techniques or elaborate spiritual practices. He simply pointed people toward the truth of how their minds actually work. He helped them see that they are not victims of their circumstances, their past, or their conditioning, but rather creators of their own experience through the power of thought.

Sydney often said that he was not teaching anything new, but rather pointing people toward what they already knew deep inside. The Three Principles, he explained, are not his principles—they are universal spiritual facts that have always existed and always will exist.

The Living Understanding

Sydney Banks passed away in 2009, but the understanding he shared contin-ues to spread and evolve. Thousands of people around the world now teach and share the Three Principles, each bringing their own unique perspective while pointing toward the same fundamental truths.

What Sydney discovered on that weekend in 1973 was not a new philosophy or psychological theory, but a direct seeing into the nature of human experience itself. The Three Principles are not concepts to be learned but truths to be realized—not through effort or study, but through the simple recognition of what is already true.

The Thought Principle, which has been the focus of this book, is just one facet of this larger understanding. But as Sydney often pointed out, you don't need to understand all three principles intellectually to benefit from them. A deep seeing into any one of them will naturally lead to an understanding of the others, because they are all aspects of the same unified truth.

The Continuing Journey

Today, the Three Principles continue to offer hope and healing to people around the world. They provide a simple, elegant explanation for how human beings can find their way back to mental health, wisdom, and well-being—not through fixing what's wrong, but through understanding what's right.

Sydney's legacy is not a set of techniques or methods, but a pointing toward the innate wisdom and resilience that exists within every human being. His gift to the world was the recognition that we are all far more powerful, wise, and whole than we have been led to believe.

The story of the Three Principles is ultimately the story of human potential—the recognition that no matter what we've experienced, no matter how lost or broken we might feel, we are never more than one insight away from remembering who we really are.

As Sydney himself often said, "We are all just one thought away from a completely different experience of life."

That thought—that insight—that moment of recognition is always available, always present, always waiting to be discovered. It's the birthright of every human being, and it's closer than we think.

Now that you have a bird's eye view of the Three Principles, let's discuss how thought creates your feelings.

* * *

Key Insights:

1. **Sydney Banks profound awakening** - He was a regular man struggling with anxiety and insecurity when he had a profound spiritual awakening in 1973.
2. **"You're not really insecure. You just think you are."** - This sparked a direct insight that his experience was being created from within, by thought—not by his circumstances.
3. **The Three Principles:** He realized there were universal spiritual principles behind all human psychological experience. These principles are called Mind, Consciousness, and Thought.
4. **Mind is the universal intelligence** behind all of life.
5. **Consciousness is the ability to be aware and experience life.**
6. **Thought is the creative energy** that shapes our individual experience.
7. **All human experience is created through thought, animated by Consciousness, and powered by Mind.** The Three Principles are inseparable—three aspects of the same energy, not separate forces.
8. **Thought is the most helpful principle.** Sydney emphasized that you don't need to understand all three equally.
9. **You don't need to manage Consciousness or control Mind**—they operate perfectly on their own.
10. **Thought is temporary** - Where people suffer is in misidentifying with their thoughts and not realizing thought is temporary and impersonal.
11. **Seeing Thought for what it is** - When people see Thought for what it is,

their suffering dissolves, and they return to their natural wellbeing.

12. **Word of The Three Principles got out** - Mental health professionals found this insight more transformative than years of therapy. Educators, business leaders, and even prison programs adopted the Principles with powerful results.

13. **The Three Principles are not techniques** or self-help strategies—they are descriptions of how life actually works.

14. **You are already complete** - The understanding invites people to see they already have wisdom, resilience, and wellbeing within them.

15. **The Principles are universal** - Sydney insisted he was pointing to something universal, not creating a new philosophy.

16. **The Principles continue to spread worldwide**, transforming lives through insight and simplicity.

17. **The central message:** you are never more than one thought away from a radically different experience of life.

18. **Most self-help teachings misrepresent thought as the villain.** You're told to fix, reframe, or control your thinking—but that reinforces the belief that thought has power over you.

3

How Thought Creates Feeling - The Only Way to Change Your Feelings At Will

"You don't feel the world. You feel your thinking about the world."

Have you ever noticed how your feelings can shift like weather patterns—sometimes sunny, sometimes stormy—even when absolutely nothing around you has changed?

One minute you're humming along, feeling pretty good about life. The next minute you're stressed, anxious, or irritated, and you can't quite put your finger on why. You look around for the culprit—did someone say something? Did something happen? But no, everything's exactly the same as it was five minutes ago.

Except for one thing: a new thought entered the room.

That's what this chapter is about. Not theory or mindset tricks or positive thinking mantras. Just one simple truth that, once you really see it, changes everything:

You feel your thinking. Always. In real time. No exceptions.

The Great Reversal

We've been taught our whole lives that experience comes from the outside in. It's so deeply embedded in our language that we don't even question it:

"You made me angry."

"That test stressed me out."

"This weather is depressing."

"That breakup destroyed me."

But here's the thing—this is completely backwards.

I learned this the hard way during what I now call "The Great Grocery Store Meltdown of 2023." Picture this: I'm standing in the cereal aisle, minding my own business, when this woman cuts in front of me with her cart. Not a big deal, right? Happens all the time.

But for some reason, I went from zero to furious in about two seconds. My jaw clenched, my shoulders tensed, and I started crafting this whole internal monologue about how rude people are these days, how nobody has manners anymore, how this was somehow representative of everything wrong with society.

Then I caught myself. I literally stopped mid-rant (thankfully it was still internal) and thought, Wait a minute. What just happened here?

The woman didn't make me angry. The cart-cutting incident didn't create my fury. My thinking about the cart-cutting incident created my fury. She was just trying to get her groceries, probably didn't even see me, and here I was constructing an entire narrative about the decline of Western civilization based on thirty seconds of cereal aisle interaction.

Same incident. Different thought. Completely different experience.

In the Three Principles, we see that experience comes from the inside-out. Always. It's not the thing that happens to you—it's your thinking about the thing.

Two people can be stuck in the exact same traffic jam. One is calm, maybe even enjoying the unexpected pause in their day, listening to music or a podcast. The other is fuming, gripping the steering wheel, blood pressure rising, mentally rehearsing all the ways this delay is going to ruin their entire day.

Same traffic. Different thoughts. Completely different realities.

The Hidden Chain Reaction

Here's how it actually works, the real chain of events that creates your experience:

```
Thought  →  Consciousness  →  Feeling  →  Behavior
```

You can't have a feeling without a thought first. Even if you don't notice the thought—and most of the time we don't—it's there, like the root system of a tree that you can't see but that's feeding everything above ground.

You don't feel the world directly. You feel your thought-made version of the world.

This was a revelation for me. I used to think I was some kind of emotional weather vane, picking up on all the "vibes" and "energy" around me. If someone was in a bad mood, I'd absorb it. If there was tension in a room, I'd feel it in my body. I thought I was just sensitive, maybe even psychic.

Turns out, I wasn't picking up on external energy at all. I was having thoughts about what I was observing, and then feeling those thoughts. The person's bad mood wasn't creating my discomfort—my thinking about their bad mood was creating my discomfort.

And the more you understand this, the less trapped you feel by circumstances, by other people's moods, by situations that used to knock you sideways.

You realize: "This feeling isn't a signal about what's happening out there. It's a signal about what's happening in my thinking right now."

The Convincing Illusion

Now, let's be crystal clear about something: we're not saying your feelings are fake or that you should just ignore them or pretend they don't matter.

Your feelings are absolutely real. They're just not telling you what you think they're telling you.

The reason this is so confusing is because of consciousness—that magical faculty that brings everything to life. Because of consciousness, every thought gets the full Hollywood treatment. It gets color, texture, sound, emotion. Your body reacts as if it's all happening right now. Your heart races, your stomach knots, your muscles tense.

But it's still... thought.

Here's what I mean: You can remember an argument from two years ago—maybe with an ex-partner or a difficult boss—and if you really get into the memory, you'll start feeling angry all over again. Your heart rate increases, your jaw clenches, you might even find yourself mentally rehearsing what you should have said.

But that argument isn't happening right now. That person might not even be in your life anymore. Nothing real is occurring in this moment except the thought-powered replay in your mind.

Or you can imagine a future problem—maybe you're worried about a medical test result or a difficult conversation you need to have—and feel anxious right now about something that hasn't happened and might never happen.

Your body doesn't know the difference between a real tiger and an imaginary tiger. It responds to both with the same fight-or-flight response. That's how convincing the illusion is.

It's like being in a dream that feels completely real until you wake up. While you're dreaming, you don't question the reality of flying through the air or having a conversation with your third-grade teacher who's somehow also a talking elephant. It all makes perfect sense until consciousness shifts and you realize, "Oh, that was just a dream."

The Moment Everything Changes

The moment you start to see this happening in real time—the moment you catch thought creating your experience—something profound shifts.

You stop fighting your feelings because you understand they're not permanent fixtures but temporary weather patterns.

You stop blaming people or situations for how you feel because you see that your experience is being generated from the inside.

You stop assuming your mood means that something is wrong with your life because you recognize it as information about your current thinking, not your circumstances.

And that space—that moment of awareness—creates freedom.

I remember the first time I really caught this in action. I was about to send what I now call "a nuclear text message" to someone who had disappointed me. You know the kind—the message you craft when you're hurt and angry, the one designed to make the other person feel as bad as you do.

I had typed out this masterpiece of passive-aggressive communication, my thumb hovering over the send button, when something made me pause. Maybe it was the intensity of the heat I felt in my chest, or the way my hands were actually shaking with anger, but suddenly I thought, Wait... this is just angry thinking. I don't actually need to act on this.

I put the phone down and went for a walk around the block. By the time I got back—maybe fifteen minutes later—the storm had completely passed. I looked at that unsent message and couldn't believe I'd been ready to send it. It felt like reading someone else's words.

I didn't control my thought. I didn't try to think positive thoughts or talk myself out of being angry. I just didn't believe the angry thinking was telling me the truth about what I needed to do in that moment. And that was enough.

29

The Natural Intelligence of Not Knowing

Once you really understand that thought creates feeling in real time, you naturally become more curious about your own experience. Instead of immediately believing every emotional weather pattern that moves through, you start to wonder:

"If this feeling is just thought... what happens if I wait?"

"What if I don't need to figure this out right now?"

"What if this mood doesn't mean what I think it means?"

You begin to notice that your moods rise and fall like tides, without needing your analysis or intervention. You stop overreacting to every emotional wave because you understand that waves, by their very nature, rise and fall.

You start to trust your system more. You realize that just like your body knows how to heal a cut without your conscious direction, your mind knows how to return to clarity without your mental management.

And from that place of not-knowing, of not needing to figure everything out, something beautiful happens. Wisdom shows up. Clarity shows up. Peace shows up.

Not because you chased them or worked for them or earned them, but because you stopped chasing anything. You created space for your natural intelligence to emerge.

Today's Simple Thought-Practice

This week, I want to offer you the simplest practice in the world. Whenever you find yourself caught in a strong feeling—anger, anxiety, sadness, frustration, whatever it is—ask yourself this question:

"Is this feeling coming from life... or from thought?"

Don't answer quickly. Don't make it into an intellectual exercise. Just sit with the question. Watch. Be curious.

You might be surprised by what you discover.

You might start to feel something far more powerful than any technique or strategy: the quiet knowing that you are the experiencer, not the experience.

That you are the sky, not the weather. That you are the theater, not the play.

And in that knowing, you'll find a freedom that no external circumstance can give you or take away.

Because when you really see that you don't feel the world—you feel your thinking about the world—everything becomes possible again.

The traffic jam becomes just a traffic jam. The difficult person becomes just a difficult person. The challenging situation becomes just a challenging situation. None of it, an existential crisis worthy of you sacrificing your peace of mind because you now know it's just thought.

And you? You become free to respond from wisdom instead of reacting from thought-created emotion.

You become free to be yourself again.

* * *

Key Insights:

- **You feel your thinking, not the world.** Emotions are responses to your internal thoughts, not direct reflections of external events. Everything felt is created within.
- **Your mood can change without your circumstances changing.** A new thought can shift your emotional state in an instant, even if nothing outside of you has changed.
- **We're conditioned to think experience is outside-in.** Phrases like "you made me mad" reflect a common but incorrect belief that people or events cause our feelings.
- **Experience is actually created from the inside-out.** Your thoughts about a situation—not the situation itself—determine how you experience it.
- **Thought always comes before feeling.** Even when unnoticed, thought is the root of every emotion. No feeling can exist without a preceding thought.
- **You don't absorb energy—you interpret it.** What feels like picking up on someone else's mood is actually your thinking about them, not their

mood itself.

- **Feelings are real, but their source may be illusory.** Your body reacts vividly to imagined scenarios or memories, but that doesn't make them true.
- **Consciousness gives thought the appearance of reality.** Thanks to consciousness, every thought seems real—complete with emotions, physical sensations, and detail.
- **Memory and imagination can feel like reality.** Thinking about the past or future can evoke powerful feelings, even though those moments aren't happening now.
- **The body reacts to thought like it's real danger.** Your nervous system can't distinguish between a real threat and a mental projection—it responds to both.
- **Recognizing thought breaks emotional spells.** The moment you see you're caught in thought, your identification with the emotion starts to dissolve.
- **You don't have to act on every thought.** Strong feelings don't require immediate reaction. Just noticing they're thought-generated creates space to choose.
- **Emotional storms pass on their own.** You don't need to fix or manage your mood. Like weather, it will shift if you let it be.
- **You're the awareness, not the emotion.** The deeper truth is that you are the observer of your thoughts and feelings—not the contents of your mind.
- **Freedom comes from seeing the source.** Once you understand your experience is being generated internally, you stop feeling like a victim of circumstance.
- **Your system is self-correcting.**
- Just as your body heals naturally, your mind can reset to peace without effort when not interfered with.
- **Wisdom arises in stillness.** When you stop trying to fix your emotions or figure them out, clarity often shows up on its own.
- **Curiosity is more helpful than control.** Asking simple questions like "Is

this coming from thought or life?" creates space for insight and ease.

· **Thought creates emotional illusion—and liberation.** Understanding that thought is the hidden creator of experience reveals the path to emotional freedom.

· **You can always return to inner peace.** You're never more than one insight away from clarity, because peace is your natural state beneath thought.

4

Feelings - The Convincing Liar

"Feeling something intensely is not evidence of truth. It's evidence of believed thought—that's all."

L et me ask you something: Have you ever believed something so strongly—with every fiber of your being—only to realize later it wasn't true at all?

Maybe it was that person you were convinced hated you, until you found out they'd been going through their own struggles and barely noticed your existence. Or that worry that kept you up at night for weeks, the one that never actually materialized. Or that story you've been telling yourself for years about not being good enough, smart enough, worthy enough—until one day you caught a glimpse of yourself through someone else's eyes and realized how distorted your self-perception had become.

We all fall for thoughts that masquerade as truth. The scary part? They don't just whisper their lies—they shout them with the full force of our emotions, our physical sensations, our entire felt experience of reality.

But that doesn't make them true.

In this chapter, we're going to explore why thoughts feel so convincing, why our minds are such skilled magicians when it comes to creating illusions, and how to wake up from the spell without needing to fight your own thinking.

The Master of Disguise

Here's what makes thought so tricky, so seductive, so damn convincing: it doesn't just talk to you. It feels to you.

When a thought shows up in your mind, it doesn't arrive like a polite suggestion you can consider at your leisure. It comes with a full sensory experience. Your body reacts. Your heart rate changes. Your muscles tense or relax. Your breathing shifts. Your emotions flood in like a tide.

So it's completely natural to assume:

"If I feel anxious, something must be wrong."

"If I feel rejected, they must not like me."

"If I feel scared, this situation must be dangerous."

"If I feel like a failure, I must actually be failing."

But here's what I've learned the hard way: thought creates a feeling, and that feeling reinforces the thought. It's a closed loop, a feedback system that can convince you of almost anything.

Let me tell you about the time I almost quit my business because of a thought that felt so true, so urgent, so undeniably real that I was ready to throw away years of work based on it.

It was a Tuesday morning—why is it always Tuesday?—and I was looking at my bank account. Business had been slow for a few weeks, which wasn't unusual, but for some reason that morning, the thought hit me like a freight train: You're failing. This whole thing is falling apart. You're not cut out for this.

Within minutes, I could feel the thought taking over my entire system. My chest tightened. My stomach dropped. My hands started shaking slightly as I began mentally calculating how long I could survive on my savings, what I would tell people when I had to shut everything down, how I would explain to my family that I'd wasted all this time chasing a dream that was never going to work.

The feeling was so intense, so visceral, so real that I started drafting emails to clients, preparing to wind down operations. I was convinced—not just intellectually, but in my bones—that this was the end.

Then my landlord walked into my office. Picture this guy: short, bald, late-middle-aged, with a voice and attitude at least twenty-four inches taller than his actual stature. He had this way of cutting through nonsense that could be either infuriating or enlightening, depending on your mood.

"How are things going?" he asked in his characteristically direct way.

Still caught in the grip of my catastrophic thinking, I replied, "Times are tough. I'm barely getting by. I'm living week to week and don't know if I'll survive the next month."

Without missing a beat, in that gruff voice that somehow managed to be both dismissive and caring at the same time, he said, "Ray, you've been one month away from closing your doors every week for the last three years."

The words hit me like a splash of cold water.

He was absolutely right. The circumstances were virtually unchanged from three years ago—hell, they were almost identical to what they'd been for most of my business journey. I'd always managed to get by. I'd always found a way to survive. The cash flow ebbed and flowed, clients came and went, but somehow, someway, I always made it through.

What was different this Tuesday morning wasn't my situation. It was that my thoughts felt real in a way they hadn't before. It actually felt like I wouldn't survive the next month, even though the evidence of my track record suggested otherwise.

In the span of a five-minute conversation, everything changed. Not my circumstances—those had been the same all along. Not my skills or my business model or my potential for success. Just my thinking.

The thought that had felt so true, so urgent, so undeniably accurate just an hour earlier suddenly seemed... ridiculous. Like waking up from a nightmare and realizing none of it was real.

The Body Doesn't Lie—Or Does It?

Your emotions are real. Let me be absolutely clear about that. When you feel anxious, sad, angry, or afraid, those feelings are genuine experiences happening in your body right now.

But the story those emotions are built on? That might be complete fiction. Feeling something intensely is not evidence of truth. It's evidence of believed thought—that's all.

Think about the last nightmare you had. In that dream, your heart was probably racing. You might have been sweating, your muscles tense with fear or the urge to run. You felt panic, terror, maybe even physical pain.

Was any of it true? Was there actually a monster chasing you, or a building collapsing, or whatever scenario your sleeping mind conjured up?

Of course not. But your body didn't know that. Your nervous system responded to the imagined threat as if it were completely real.

That's exactly how thought works when we're awake. The mind plays a movie—sometimes a horror film, sometimes a tragedy, sometimes a thriller where you're the victim. Consciousness lights it up, makes it vivid and compelling and emotionally charged. You feel it in your body with the same intensity as if it were actually happening.

But it's still just... a movie.

The Stories We Tell Ourselves

Let me share some real-life examples of how this plays out, because I guarantee you've experienced one or more of these scenarios:

You send a text to someone important to you and don't hear back for a few hours. The thought pops up: "They're ignoring me. They're mad at me. I must have said something wrong." Within minutes, you feel rejected, anxious, maybe even angry. You start crafting defensive responses or planning how you'll handle the confrontation. Turns out, they were in back-to-back meetings all day and didn't even see your message.

You walk into a room full of people—maybe a party, a work event, a social gathering. The thought hits: "Everyone's looking at me. They're judging me. They can tell I don't belong here." Your face flushes, your palms sweat, you want to hide in the bathroom or leave entirely. In reality, most people are so caught up in their own conversations and concerns that they barely registered your entrance.

You have a slow week in your business, or get some critical feedback, or make a mistake. The thought arrives with devastating certainty: "I'm not cut out for this. I'm a fraud. Everyone's going to find out I have no idea what I'm doing." You feel like a failure, like you should quit while you're ahead, like you've been fooling yourself all along. Two days later, you close a big deal or receive glowing praise from a client, and suddenly you remember why you love what you do.

Notice the pattern? Nothing external changed between the moment of despair and the moment of clarity. The circumstances were the same. The other people were the same. The only thing that shifted was the thought you were believing.

The Tinted Glasses

Thought is like wearing a pair of tinted glasses. If you forget you're wearing them, the whole world looks that color. Everything you see gets filtered through that particular lens, and you assume that's just how reality looks.

But the moment you remember—"Oh, wait, I'm wearing colored glasses"—everything starts to shift. You don't have to take the glasses off or fight with them or analyze why you put them on in the first place. You just remember that what you're seeing is being filtered, and that awareness alone changes your relationship to the experience.

"I'm a failure" → That's a thought, not a fact.

"They don't love me" → That's a thought, not a fact.

"This will never get better" → That's a thought, not a fact.

"I'm not good enough" → That's a thought, not a fact.

None of these thoughts are true just because they feel familiar. None of them are false just because they're uncomfortable. They're just... thoughts. Mental events. Temporary visitors in the hotel of your consciousness.

I learned this lesson in the most unexpected way on my first day of university. I walked into that school carrying a thought I'd believed for every one of my preceding twenty-one years: I am an introvert.

Picture the scene: a massive lecture hall filled with over a hundred other students, all of us there for orientation to what was supposedly a highly competitive program. I found a seat somewhere in the middle, trying to make myself invisible, feeling that familiar cocktail of insecurity and fear that had been my companion through most of my educational journey.

I hadn't met anyone in the class yet, and frankly, I felt like I was probably the dumbest person in the room. I'm not exaggerating when I say I thought someone had made a mistake letting me into this program. Surely they'd figure it out soon enough and send me packing.

The thought that took hold was crystal clear and felt absolutely true: I'm an introvert. No one is going to want to talk to me. I'm going to sit here in silence for the next four years, invisible and alone.

This thought felt so real, so urgent, so backed up by twenty-one years of evidence that I could feel myself sinking into that familiar socially depressed state. My shoulders hunched forward, my breathing became shallow, and I started mentally preparing for another few years of social isolation.

The anxiety from this thinking made me feel worse, which reinforced the thought that I was fundamentally different from everyone else, that I was destined to be the quiet one in the corner. It was a perfect storm of thought creating feeling creating more thought, each cycle making the "truth" of my introversion feel more solid, more permanent.

Then, out of absolutely nowhere, a different thought popped into my head: Nobody here knows I'm an introvert. For all they know, I could be the most personable, outgoing guy they've ever met.

It was such a simple shift, but it hit me like lightning. I realized I'd been so focused on my past behavior, so committed to the story I'd been telling about myself, that I'd forgotten something crucial: I was in a completely new environment with completely new people. My history didn't have to be my destiny.

I'd been wearing these "introvert" glasses for so long that I couldn't see any other reality. But suddenly, sitting in that lecture hall, I caught a glimpse of what might be possible if I took them off.

Before I could talk myself out of it—before my rational mind could remind me of all the reasons why this was a terrible idea—something possessed my body. I stood up, walked to the front of the class, and stepped up to the lectern microphone.

My heart was pounding so hard I was sure everyone could hear it, but I opened my mouth and said, "Hi everybody, my name is Ray, and I feel like we should come together as a class. Here's what I want to do."

I pointed to one half of the room. "This side, you're going to say 'Mufasa!'" Then I pointed to the other half. "And this side, you're going to respond with 'Ooooooh, say it again!'" (Yes, straight from The Lion King—don't ask me where that came from.)

For a moment, there was complete silence. I stood there thinking, Well, this is it. This is how I become known as the weird guy who made a Lion King reference on the first day.

But then, much to my absolute amazement, everyone played along. For the next three minutes, the lecture hall erupted in this ridiculous call-and-response, with half the class shouting "Mufasa!" and the other half responding with "Ooooooh, say it again!" People were laughing, clapping, some even standing up to get more dramatic with their delivery.

From that moment on, I was known as Ray—the extroverted, charismatic guy in the class. Not the introvert. Not the quiet one. The guy who could get a hundred strangers to participate in a Lion King sing-along within the first hour of meeting them.

My past was real. The twenty-one years of quiet behavior, the social anxiety, the preference for staying in the background—all of that had actually happened. But the story I'd built around those experiences, the meaning I'd assigned to them, the identity I'd constructed from them—that was just thought.

And thoughts, as it turns out, can change in an instant.

I want to be clear about something before we move on, I'm not suggesting that you change your thought, I'm inviting you simply to see that it's all thought! See that the "introvert thought" was just thought and the "extrovert thought" was just thought too.

The Freedom in Seeing

When you start to see thought as thought rather than as truth, something remarkable happens. You don't have to fight your thinking or try to replace "negative" thoughts with "positive" ones. You don't have to analyze where the thoughts came from or why you're having them.

You just remember: "Oh, this is thinking. This is my mind doing what minds do—creating stories, making meaning, trying to figure everything out."

And in that remembering, you create space. Space between you and the thought. Space between the thought and your reaction to it. Space for something else to emerge—maybe wisdom, maybe peace, maybe just a lighter way of being with whatever's happening.

This doesn't mean you ignore practical concerns or dismiss genuine intuition. It means you stop mistaking the voice in your head for the voice of truth. You stop assuming that because something feels urgent, it must be important. You stop believing that because something feels real, it must be accurate.

You start to trust something deeper than thought—the part of you that exists before the story, underneath the narrative, beyond the mental commentary.

That part of you that knows, without thinking, what's true.

The Simple Thought-Practice of Gentle Skepticism

This week, I want to invite you to become a gentle skeptic of your own thinking. Not cynical, not dismissive, just... curious.

When a thought shows up with a lot of emotional charge—when it feels urgent and true and demands immediate action—pause for just a moment and ask:

"Is this thought, or is this truth?"

"What if this feeling is just the result of a story I'm telling myself?"

"What would I see if I weren't wearing these particular glasses right now?"

You don't have to answer these questions. You don't have to figure anything out. Just asking them creates a little space, a small gap between you and the thought.

And in that gap, you might discover something beautiful: you are not your thoughts. You are the awareness in which thoughts arise and pass away.

You are not the movie. You are the screen on which all movies are projected.

And from that place of knowing, you can watch even the most convincing illusions with a sense of wonder rather than fear, curiosity rather than belief.

Because when you really see that thoughts are just thoughts—not facts, not commands, not prophecies—you become free to respond to life from wisdom rather than react from the stories in your head.

And that, my friend, changes everything.

* * *

Key Insights:

- **Feeling something deeply doesn't make it true.** Intense emotion is not a sign of accuracy—it's a sign that a thought is being believed.
- **Thoughts feel real because they come with a full-body experience.** When you believe a thought, your nervous system reacts as if what you're thinking is real.
- **The loop of thought and feeling is self-reinforcing.** Thought creates feeling, and feeling strengthens belief in the original thought, forming a convincing cycle.
- **You can be totally wrong and still feel totally certain.** Our strongest feelings often come from our most unquestioned assumptions—not necessarily from facts.
- **Your body responds to imagined threats like real ones.** Just like in a nightmare, your physical reaction doesn't mean the danger is real—it just means the mind is active.
- **Thought is like a dream that feels real until you wake up.** When believed,

thought creates a full sensory illusion that feels true until awareness breaks the spell.

· **Your situation doesn't have to change for your experience to shift.** When your thinking changes, your reality changes—even if nothing around you has.

· **Seeing thought as thought dissolves its power.** The moment you realize "this is just a thought," it loses its grip and stops running the show.

· **Stories about yourself are just mental habits.** Labels like "introvert" or "failure" aren't fixed truths—they're repeated thoughts you've come to believe.

· **Identity is fluid when thought is seen clearly.** Even long-held beliefs about who you are can shift in a moment when you stop identifying with them.

· **Urgency is not the same as importance.** Just because a thought feels urgent doesn't mean it demands action—it just means it's charged with emotion.

· **All thoughts are temporary visitors.** No matter how compelling they seem, every thought eventually passes—none are permanent truths.

· **The more real a thought feels, the more gently you should question it.** When thinking feels most gripping, it's a sign to pause and ask if it's actually true.

· **Awareness is the space between you and the story.** You're not the narrator in your head—you're the presence that notices the narration.

· **You don't need to fix thoughts—just see them.** Freedom doesn't come from changing thought, but from recognizing it for what it is.

· **You are not your thoughts—you're the awareness behind them.** Thoughts come and go, but the observer—the conscious awareness you are—remains constant and untouched.

· **Gentle skepticism is more powerful than positive thinking.** Instead of forcing optimism, quietly asking "Is this true?" can open the door to clarity.

· **Seeing through thought reveals deeper wisdom.** When you're not caught in mental stories, something more grounded and intelligent can guide you.

- **Even lifelong beliefs can change in a moment.** All it takes is one glimpse of awareness to unravel a decades-old story.
- **There's nothing to fight—just something to notice.** You don't have to push back against thought. Noticing it's thought is enough to reclaim your peace.

5

The Temporary Nature of Thought and Why Doing Nothing Often Trumps Doing Everything

"Thought doesn't stay unless you hold on to it."

L et me guess... you're tired of thinking so much. Tired of that relentless mental chatter that starts the moment you wake up and follows you around like a shadow all day. Tired of feeling stuck in the same loops, wrestling with the same worries, having the same arguments with yourself that you had yesterday and the day before and the day before that.

Tired of your own mind.

I get it. I've been there—lying awake at 3 AM, my brain spinning like a washing machine stuck on the agitation cycle, churning through every possible scenario of how things could go wrong, replaying conversations from five years ago, planning arguments with people who probably aren't even thinking about me.

What if I told you that the thoughts that haunt you were never meant to stay? What if thought is just passing weather, but you've been trying to build your house in the middle of a storm?

This chapter is about one realization that brings profound relief—the kind of relief you feel when you finally understand something that's been confusing you for years:

```
Thought is temporary. Always. No matter how intense, how painful,
or how convincingly real it feels--it doesn't last.
```

The One Thing You Need to Know

If you learn one thing from this entire book, let it be this: Thought always moves. The only question is—will you let it?

Think about your own mind for a moment. Really think about it.

You've had thoughts that felt absolutely, unshakably true at 2 AM— thoughts about your worth, your future, your relationships—that seemed laughable by 8 AM when you'd had some coffee and perspective.

You've been crushed by memories one day, feeling like they might swallow you whole, and then been completely numb to those same memories the next day, wondering why they ever bothered you.

You've gone from confident to insecure to neutral in the span of a few hours, with no external change whatsoever. Nothing in your life shifted, no new information came in, no one said anything different to you.

What changed? Not your life. Not your situation. Not your circumstances.

Your thinking. That's all.

I remember a period in my life when I was convinced I was having what people politely call "a quarter-life crisis" but what felt more like a complete existential meltdown. I was twenty-five, preparing to graduate college and faced with a decision that felt like it would determine the entire trajectory of my life: do I take a job where I'd make good money but likely be miserable, or do I sell my Subaru and use the money to start a business in the basement of a friend's house?

Every morning I'd wake up with this crushing weight on my chest, this certainty that I was standing at a crossroads and any step I took would be the wrong one.

The thoughts were relentless: What do you know about starting a business? Every day that you don't make a decision, the best jobs are being scooped up by your graduating classmates. You're broke, and if you make the wrong decision, you could be even more broke. Everyone else has it figured out. You're behind. You're failing. You'll never find your purpose. Who are you kidding? You're fundamentally broken.

These thoughts felt so real, so true, so permanent that I started making major life decisions based on them. I was ready to take a job doing something I knew I'd hate—anything to escape the prison of my own thinking.

But then something interesting happened. I got the flu.

For three days, I was so sick I couldn't think about anything except getting through the next hour. I couldn't worry about my future or analyze my past or compare myself to anyone else. I just existed, moment by moment, focused on the simple tasks of staying hydrated and getting rest.

When I finally recovered, something had shifted. Those thoughts that had felt so urgent, so true, so permanent just a week earlier? They were still there, but they felt... lighter. Less solid. Like clouds that had lost their storm potential.

Nothing in my external life had changed. I still had the same decision to make, the same financial constraints, the same uncertainty about the future. But my thinking had moved, the way weather moves, and suddenly everything looked different.

The decision that had felt impossible became clear. Not because I'd figured anything out, but because I'd stopped trying to figure everything out.

The Problem Isn't the Thoughts

Here's the twist that took me years to understand: Thought isn't the problem. It's our relationship to thought that creates suffering.

Most people—and I was definitely one of them—approach unwanted thoughts like they're enemy combatants that need to be defeated:

We argue with our thoughts, trying to logic our way out of them.

We fixate on them, analyzing them from every angle, trying to understand where they came from and what they mean.

We try to reframe them or fight them or replace them with "better" thoughts. There were many days I stomped confidently around the neighborhood repeating in my head, "Day by day in every way I'm getting better and better!".

But here's what I've learned: thought was always designed to pass through, not stick around and set up permanent residence.

Think of it like a cloud moving across the sky. Clouds don't get stuck up there unless something interferes with the natural flow of air currents. They move, they change, they dissolve and reform and move some more.

But what if you tried to trap a cloud in a jar? What if you spent all your energy trying to capture it, control it, analyze its composition, predict its movements?

You'd miss the simple beauty of watching it pass.

The more personally you take your thoughts, the longer they linger. The more you try to fix them, the louder they get. It's like trying to smooth out wrinkles in water—the more you interfere, the more disturbance you create.

The Snow Globe Mind

Let me share a metaphor that changed everything for me.

Imagine your mind is like one of those snow globes you had as a kid. When you shake it, the flakes swirl around in a chaotic storm. You can't see the little scene inside clearly—everything is obscured by the movement, the agitation.

But when you stop shaking it and just set it down, something magical happens. The snow begins to settle. Slowly, gently, without any effort on your part, clarity returns. The scene becomes visible again.

That's your mind.

You don't need to shake it less—thoughts will come, that's what minds do. You don't need to force the snow down or try to control where each flake lands.

You just stop stirring.

And when you do, the most amazing thing happens: Sadness softens. Worry fades. Insight arises. Peace returns.

Not because you "did the work" or earned it or figured something out. Because you stopped interfering with a system that already knows how to reset itself.

I learned this during what I now call "The Great Overthinking Experiment of 2010." I had been struggling with a decision about whether to buy out my business partner after the partnership had gone south. For months, I analyzed every angle, made pro-and-con lists, sought advice from everyone I knew, researched until my eyes burned.

The more I thought about it, the more confused I became. Every day brought new considerations, new fears, new what-ifs. I was drowning in my own analysis.

Finally, exhausted by my own mental gymnastics, I decided to take a week off from thinking about it entirely. Not because I had some grand strategy, but because I literally couldn't think about it anymore without feeling like my head might explode.

I went to Florida. Turned the phone off, no internet, no way to research or analyze or seek more input. Just me, sun, an ocean, and the simple rhythm of walking on the beach and reading books.

By the third day, something had shifted. Not because I'd figured anything out, but because I'd stopped trying to figure anything out. The mental snow globe had settled, and suddenly I could see clearly again.

The answer wasn't in all that thinking. It was underneath it, waiting patiently for the storm to pass.

The Illusion of Forever

"But what if I keep having the same thought over and over?" you might ask. "What if it feels like I'm stuck in a loop that never ends?"

Late author and spiritual teacher, Wayne Dyer, use to refer to this situation as "the turd that wouldn't flush", he'd say, "it just circles the bowl over and over again, but just won't go down."

I hear you. Some thoughts do seem to have frequent-flyer status in our minds, showing up again and again like unwelcome house guests who don't know when to leave.

But here's something that might surprise you: even when it feels like you're having the same thought repeatedly, you're actually having a series of new thoughts that happen to have similar content. Each one is fresh, arising in this moment, and each one has the same temporary nature as every other thought.

It's like waves on the ocean. From a distance, it might look like the same wave hitting the shore over and over. But each wave is unique, formed by different currents, carrying different water, lasting for its own brief moment before dissolving back into the sea.

Every single thought—even the ones that feel familiar, even the ones that seem to define you—is:

Not you. Not the ultimate truth. Not permanent.

The thought might say, "You'll always feel this way." But that too is just another thought, with no more permanence or authority than any other.

And here's the strange irony I've discovered: the moment you stop believing the thought that says "This will never end" is often the moment it begins to end.

Today's Simple Thought-Practice - Letting Weather Pass

Here's what I want to offer you—not as another technique to master or strategy to implement, but as a gentle experiment in being human:

The next time you feel overwhelmed, anxious, or stuck in a thought storm, pause. Just for a moment.

Instead of asking your usual questions—"How do I fix this? What does this mean? Why do I keep thinking this? What's wrong with me?"—try asking this:

```
"What if this thought is just passing through?"
```

You might not feel better right away. That's not the point. But you might feel less gripped, less at the mercy of whatever's moving through your mental space.

And that small shift—from being trapped by thought to watching thought—creates space. And in that space, something beautiful happens.

Thought starts to move again, the way it was always meant to.

Insight arises, not from your effort but from your willingness to stop efforting.

Peace begins to return, not because you've solved anything but because you've stopped trying to solve everything.

Wisdom gets a chance to speak, in the quiet moments between the mental noise.

The Weather Report

I want to leave you with this image: You are not the weather. You are the sky.

Storms pass through you—sometimes gentle spring showers, sometimes fierce thunderstorms that seem like they might tear you apart. But you are not the storm. You are the vast, unchanging space in which all weather occurs.

Thoughts are like clouds, feelings like wind patterns, moods like seasonal changes. They all move through the sky of your being, but they are not you.

This week, I invite you to notice your thoughts—not to judge them or fix them or make them better, but just to see how temporary they really are.

Let one pass. Then another. Watch them come and go like cars on a highway, each one heading somewhere else, none of them your permanent address.

And when you find yourself spiraling, caught in the grip of thinking that feels too big, too real, too permanent, just whisper this to yourself:

"It's just weather. And weather never stays."

Because it doesn't. It never has, and it never will.

The storm you're in right now? It's already changing, already moving, already beginning to pass.

You just have to stop trying to hold onto it.

* * *

Key Insights:

- **Thought is always temporary.** No matter how intense or convincing it feels, every thought is like weather—designed to pass through, not stay.
- **The mind naturally resets—if we let it.** Like a snow globe settling, clarity returns when we stop stirring the mind with constant analysis or resistance.
- **You don't need to fix thought—just stop holding it.** Trying to control or fight thoughts often keeps them alive; letting them pass brings peace.
- **What feels overwhelming now may feel light tomorrow.** Thoughts that seem unbearable in one moment can feel irrelevant just a few hours later, proving their impermanence.
- **Thought itself isn't the problem—gripping it is.** Suffering arises not from having thoughts, but from believing, resisting, or identifying with them.
- **Every moment is a fresh thought, not a repeating loop.** Even recurring worries are new thoughts with old content—they only seem the same when we mistake them for facts.
- **Efforting blocks insight.** Clarity doesn't come from pushing harder—it arises naturally when the noise settles and space opens up.
- **Thought moves when you stop interfering.** Letting go of the need to analyze, fix, or manage your mind allows thought to flow again, as it was meant to.
- **Trying to "figure it out" keeps you stuck.** Mental overprocessing is like shaking the snow globe—it clouds the view rather than clarifying it.
- **Emotional intensity isn't evidence of truth.** Strong feelings reflect believed thoughts—not the reality of a situation or your identity.
- **Believed thought creates artificial urgency.** When you believe a thought,

it demands immediate action or resolution—even when no real crisis exists.

· **Peace comes not from solving, but from seeing.** Freedom happens when you realize the storm is just passing weather, not a problem to fix.

· **Letting thought be temporary creates space for wisdom.** You don't have to generate insight—it naturally emerges in the space left by passing thoughts.

· **Every thought is like a wave—it rises, crests, and dissolves.** Even the most painful or obsessive thoughts lose power when seen as transient energy.

· **You are the sky, not the storm.** Thoughts and moods move through you, but they are not you—they're momentary experiences in awareness.

· **Stopping the chase allows resolution.** The moment you stop trying to escape or fix thought, it often resolves on its own.

· **You're not behind—you're just caught in a thought storm.** What feels like failure or inadequacy is often just weathered thinking passing through.

· **Trying to control thought is like trapping clouds.** The more you chase or grasp, the more stuck thought becomes—freedom comes from watching it pass.

· **Weather never stays. Neither does thought.** No matter how heavy or persistent it seems, thought always moves—your job is simply to let it.

6

Finding Your Center - The One Who Sees

"You are not your thoughts. You are the one who sees them come... and go."

L et's slow this down for a moment.

There's something I want to tell you that might change the way you experience yourself forever. It's simple, but it's also revolutionary. It's something that, once you really see it, can't be unseen.

Ready?

Here it is: You are not your thoughts.

Not the loud ones that keep you awake at night. Not the scary ones that make your heart race. Not the broken ones that whisper you're not enough. Not even the brilliant ones that make you feel clever or special.

You are the awareness that sees them all.

And that, my friend, is the safest place you'll ever find.

The Great Misunderstanding

Most people believe they are their thoughts. Listen to how we talk:

"I'm anxious." "I'm a failure." "I'm not enough." "I'm broken." "I'm the overthinker." "I'm not enough"

But what if that's not true? What if those are just labels—temporary visitors made of passing thought? What if the real you has never changed, never been damaged, never been anything other than whole?

This might sound like spiritual fluff, but stick with me. Because understanding this distinction—between you and your thoughts—is the difference between being tossed around by every mental storm and standing in the calm center of your own being.

Thought Isn't Personal—It's Weather

Let's get something straight right off the bat: You don't choose most of your thoughts. They just show up, uninvited, like weather.

You didn't choose to think about that embarrassing thing you said three years ago that suddenly popped into your mind while you were brushing your teeth this morning.

You didn't ask to imagine that worst-case scenario about your relationship, your job, your health, your future.

You didn't invent that voice that says you're not smart enough, not attractive enough, not successful enough.

These thoughts just... appeared. Like clouds forming in the sky.

And if you didn't ask for a thought, if you didn't consciously create it, why would you assume it's you?

I learned this lesson in the most mundane way possible. I was sitting in a coffee shop, minding my own business, working on my laptop, when suddenly this thought popped into my head: Everyone here thinks you're a loser sitting alone.

Now, I hadn't been thinking about the other people in the coffee shop. I wasn't feeling particularly insecure that day. The thought just arrived, fully formed, like someone had dropped it into my mental inbox.

For a split second, I started to believe it. I felt that familiar tightness in my chest, that urge to pack up and leave, that self-consciousness that makes you hyper-aware of every movement you make.

But then I caught myself and thought, Wait a minute. Where did that even come from? I was just thinking about work, and suddenly I'm worried about what strangers think of me?

That's when it hit me: thoughts aren't personal. They're not mine in the way my hands are mine or my memories are mine. They're more like radio stations—sometimes you tune into a clear, pleasant frequency, sometimes you get static, sometimes you pick up someone else's signal entirely.

Thoughts are weather patterns of the mind. Some stormy, some sunny, all temporary.

The Quiet Witness

If you've ever had a moment of clarity—and I know you have—you already know what I'm talking about.

That split second where you realize, "Oh... I'm watching this thought, not being consumed by it."

That moment when you step back from the mental drama and think, "Wow, my mind is really going crazy right now."

That awareness that can observe your own thinking? That's you. The real you.

You're not the thinker. You're the one aware of thinking happening.

There's a voice in your head narrating everything—commenting, judging, analyzing, worrying, planning. But there's also a quiet awareness watching that voice, like someone sitting in a theater watching a movie.

That awareness is what you actually are.

Think about it: If you can observe a thought, it can't be you. Just like you can observe your emotions without being your emotions, you can observe your body without being your body, you can observe your thoughts without being your thoughts.

These things—thoughts, feelings, sensations—come and go. They change constantly. But the awareness that perceives them? That remains constant. That's your true home.

I remember the first time I really got this. I was going through a particularly difficult period, caught in what felt like an endless loop of anxious thinking.

Every day brought new worries, new catastrophic scenarios, new reasons to believe that everything was falling apart.

One morning, I was sitting in meditation—not because I was particularly spiritual, but because someone had told me it might help with the continuous, circular thinking—when suddenly I had this strange experience. It was like I stepped back from my own mind and could see all the anxious thoughts swirling around like a tornado.

But I wasn't in the tornado. I was watching it from a place of complete stillness.

For the first time in weeks, I felt peace. Not because the thoughts had stopped—they were still there, still spinning—but because I realized I wasn't them. I was the space in which they were happening.

That's when I understood: I'm not the storm. I'm the sky it's passing through.

The Identity Trap

Here's where it gets really interesting. We don't just believe our thoughts—we build entire identities out of them.

"I'm the anxious one in the family." "I'm the achiever who never feels satisfied." "I'm the one who always messes things up." "I'm the perfectionist." "I'm the people-pleaser." "I'm the one who can't commit."

But these aren't who you are. These are just repeated thoughts, believed over time, that have crystallized into what feels like a solid sense of self.

```
Identity, when you really look at it, is just memory plus
thought. Nothing more.
```

You remember past experiences, you think about what they mean, you create a story about who you are based on those interpretations, and then you live as if that story is the truth.

But if thought is temporary—and we've established that it is—then so is your story of "me."

This was a hard pill for me to swallow. I had spent years crafting what I thought was a pretty solid sense of who I was. I was "the creative one," "the sensitive one," "the one who thinks too much." These labels felt important, like they gave me a place in the world, a way to understand myself.

But I started to notice something: these identities were also prisons. Being "the sensitive one" meant I had to be careful around conflict. Being "the creative one" meant I couldn't be practical or business-minded. Being "the overthinker" meant I was stuck in analysis paralysis.

What if none of these labels were actually true? What if they were just thoughts I'd believed for so long that they felt real?

Who was I underneath all the stories? That, it turns out, is one of the most important questions to answer.

The Freedom of Not-Knowing

When you stop believing your thoughts are you, something remarkable happens. You don't become a blank slate or lose your personality. You don't go numb or become indifferent.

You go free.

You become less reactive because you're not taking every thought person-ally.

You judge yourself less because you realize there's no fixed "self" to judge.

You respond with more compassion because you see that everyone is just dealing with their own weather patterns of thought.

You stop trying to fix the "self" that never really existed in the first place.

And what fills the space that all that mental effort used to occupy?

Presence. Stillness. Clarity. Insight. And often, a deep, inexplicable love— not for any particular reason, but just because love is what's there when you stop covering it up with stories.

Not because you worked for these qualities or earned them, but because you stopped covering them up with the constant noise of mental self-improvement.

I used to spend so much energy trying to fix myself. I had lists of things I needed to work on, patterns I needed to break, aspects of my personality I needed to improve. I was like a mechanic constantly tinkering with a car that was never quite running right.

But when I started to see that there was no fixed "self" to fix, that what I thought was "me" was just a collection of temporary thoughts and stories, everything relaxed.

I didn't need to fix the anxious thoughts—they were just weather. I didn't need to overcome the insecure thoughts—they were just weather. I didn't need to improve the self-critical thoughts—they were just weather.

Weather passes. It always has, and it always will.

Today's Simple Thought-Practice - Remember Who You Are

Here's what I want to offer you as a gentle way of remembering who you really are:

This week, whenever you notice a difficult thought—whenever your mind gets loud with worry or criticism or fear—just pause for a moment and ask:

"Is this me... or is this just thought passing through?"

You don't have to answer the question. You don't have to analyze it or figure it out. Just asking creates space. And in that space, something shifts.

Sometimes I'll catch myself in the middle of a mental spiral and literally say out loud, "That's not me. That's a thought."

It sounds simple, maybe even silly, but it works. It's like stepping out of a movie theater and remembering that what you were watching was just a film, not reality.

The thought might still be there, but you're no longer lost in it. You're no longer confusing it for who you are.

The Sky and the Weather

I want to leave you with this image, because it's helped me more than any other metaphor I've encountered:

`You are not the weather. You are the sky.`

Storms pass through you—sometimes gentle spring showers of melancholy, sometimes fierce thunderstorms of anxiety or anger that seem like they might tear you apart. But you are not the storm. You are the vast, unchanging space in which all weather occurs.

Thoughts are like clouds, emotions like wind patterns, moods like seasonal changes. They all move through the sky of your being, but they are not you.

I used to live with the identity "I'm the guy who's always optimistic." It became part of how I saw myself and how others saw me. But there were days when I'd wake up feeling down for no particular reason—not because anything bad had happened, not because I was facing any particular challenge, just a gray mood that seemed to settle over me like morning fog.

On those days, I would hide it. After all, I was supposed to be the positive one, the upbeat guy who always saw the bright side. Sometimes I would try to positive-talk my way out of it, forcing myself to think grateful thoughts or reminding myself of all the good things in my life. Other times I would analyze it obsessively: "What's making me feel this way? What's wrong? What do I need to fix?"

Then I realized something liberating: there's no reason for it. It's just a weather pattern moving through the sky of my consciousness.

I discovered that if I just let the melancholy be there without fighting it, without trying to understand it or change it, it would naturally pass. Usually by the next morning, I'd feel great again—not because I had done anything to fix myself, but because moods, like weather, are temporary by nature.

I also stopped hiding these feelings from my wife. Now, when I notice that gray mood settling in, I simply tell her, "I'm having a day of melancholy." No explanation, no apology, no analysis of what might have caused it. It's just a passing mood, like announcing that it's raining outside.

Somehow, this simple acknowledgment—accepting it for what it is and releasing any need to justify or change it—transforms the entire experience. The melancholy becomes just one more object in my awareness, like noticing the sound of traffic or the feeling of my feet on the ground. The day of uninvited, uncaused melancholy arrives and passes without touching my fundamental peace of mind.

This is what I mean when I say you are the sky, not the weather. The weather doesn't define the sky, damage the sky, or change the essential nature of the sky. It simply moves through, doing what weather does, while the sky remains vast, open, and unchanged.

The sky is never damaged by the weather. It's never made dirty by the clouds or broken by the lightning. It simply provides the space for all of it to happen.

That's what you are—that spacious awareness in which all of life's experiences unfold.

This week, whenever your mind gets loud—whenever the weather gets intense—just remember:

"This is just a voice. I don't have to believe it. I'm not the storm—I'm the sky it's passing through."

And in that remembering, you'll find something that no thought can give you and no thought can take away: the unshakeable peace of knowing who you really are.

You are not your thoughts. You are the one who sees them come and go.

And that awareness—that's the safest, most loving place you'll ever find.

* * *

Key Insights:

- **You are not your thoughts.** Thoughts arise within you, but they are not you—they're temporary, passing experiences in awareness.
- **Awareness is your true self.** The real you is the one who notices thoughts, not the content of the thoughts themselves.
- **Most thoughts aren't chosen.** They appear spontaneously, like weather or static on a radio—not as a result of conscious decision-making.
- **Thoughts feel personal, but they aren't.** They often masquerade as "truth," but they're just mental events passing through your consciousness.
- **You can observe your thoughts.** If you can notice a thought, that proves you're not identical to it—there's a you that's separate from the mental chatter.
- **Identities are made of repeated thoughts.** Labels like "I'm anxious" or "I'm not good enough" are just stories built from thinking, not fixed truths.
- **You don't need to fix your thoughts.** Trying to "fix" thought often keeps it around longer; seeing through it allows it to move on.
- **The quieter witness always remains.** Beneath the mental storm is a still, observing presence that never changes or gets damaged.
- **Moods don't define you.** Like weather, feelings pass through. They're not evidence of who you are or what your life means.
- **Even recurring thoughts are new.** They may feel repetitive, but each instance is freshly arising in the present moment.
- **You don't need to justify how you feel.** You can acknowledge your inner weather without explanation—like saying, "It's cloudy today."
- **You are the sky, not the weather.** Thoughts and emotions move through you, but they don't alter the fundamental spaciousness of your awareness.
- **Letting go creates freedom.** When you stop identifying with thought, a deep sense of peace and clarity naturally emerges.
- **Mental self-improvement is often unnecessary.** Much of what we try to "fix" in ourselves is based on mistaken identity with thought, not reality.

- **Peace is found in awareness, not thought.** Unshakable peace comes from knowing you are the space where life happens—not the noise that passes through it.

7

Why Knowledge Isn't Enough to Change You

"Insight is the only thing that truly changes us—because it shows us what was always true."

One evening I was watching TV with my wife when she started sharing about a challenge she was facing at work. Being a man—and more specifically, being a man who had read every self-help book ever written—I was immediately ready with advice. I offered solutions, strategies, frameworks, and perspectives drawn from my vast library of personal development knowledge.

But she wasn't buying it. In fact, she disagreed with my entire approach to the situation.

I was insulted. Here I was, offering wisdom gleaned from years of study, and she was dismissing it. Forgetting every lesson about humility I'd ever learned, I said with more than a little indignation, "Sheri, I have read more books about psychology, personal development, and success in a week than most people read in a year. I attend more conferences and seminars on how to up-level myself and my life in a year than most people attend in a lifetime."

She looked at me with that particular expression wives reserve for moments when their husbands are being especially ridiculous, and replied with devastating simplicity: "How's that working out for you?"

In what felt like a lightning bolt of humility sent directly from the universe, I heard myself reply, "I'm the least successful person I know."

The words came out of my mouth before my mind could stop them, and in that moment, I saw something that all my reading and studying had never shown me: I had accumulated an enormous amount of intellectual knowledge, but I had virtually no insight.

I could quote chapter and verse from dozens of books about happiness, but I wasn't particularly happy. I could recite principles of success from memory, but I felt like I was constantly struggling. I had theories about peace of mind, but my mind was anything but peaceful.

All that information—all those books, seminars, conferences, and courses—had given me a sophisticated vocabulary for describing problems, but they hadn't actually solved any of them. I had become an expert in the theory of transformation without experiencing much actual transformation.

That moment with my wife was my first real taste of what insight actually feels like—not the accumulation of more knowledge, but a sudden seeing that changes everything in an instant.

You've probably been taught that change takes hard work. That transformation requires strategies, step-by-step plans, discipline, and relentless effort to think differently or feel better. That you need to grind your way to a new version of yourself through sheer force of will.

But what if real change happens in an instant?

Not because you tried to change, not because you followed the right program or read the right book or implemented the perfect system, but because you saw something new. Because in one moment of clarity, everything shifted.

In this chapter, we're exploring the only thing that actually transforms us at the deepest level—and it's not mindset hacks, positive affirmations, or behavioral modifications.

It's insight. A fresh realization that arises not from effort, but from quiet clarity. A moment when the fog lifts and you see what was always there, waiting to be discovered.

The Lightning Strike

Insight is a moment of realization that comes from beyond your thinking. It's not solving a puzzle with your intellect. It's not an analytical breakthrough where you connect the dots through careful reasoning. It's not logic working its way to a conclusion.

```
It's seeing something you didn't see before--and suddenly,
everything shifts.
```

You don't figure out insight. It finds you when you're not looking.

Think about the last time you suddenly understood something in a completely new way. Maybe it was about a relationship that had been confusing you, or a pattern in your life that you'd been struggling with, or even something as simple as why a joke was funny.

You didn't build your way there through careful analysis. You weren't trying to have a breakthrough. It just... landed. Like lightning striking on a clear day.

One moment you didn't see it, and the next moment you did. And once you saw it, you couldn't unsee it. The understanding became part of you, woven into the fabric of how you experience reality.

That's insight.

I remember the exact moment I understood the difference between thought and thinking. I was watching a video of a coach walking a woman through an exercise designed to help her experience this distinction firsthand. Now, I'll admit it—I'm an information junkie. I watch a lot of videos, read countless books, consume content like it's my job. But this time was different.

Instead of just passively watching, I decided to participate. As the coach asked the woman questions, I pretended he was asking me and answered out loud, right there, standing at my treadmill desk in my home office.

"Close your eyes," he said to her. So I closed mine.

"Do you notice any sounds in your environment?" he asked.

I listened carefully, as if he was coaching me, and answered aloud, "Yes, I hear children talking."

"Did it require any effort to hear the sound (the children talking), or did it happen without any effort?"

I paused, really considering this. "It didn't require effort," I replied. "The sound was just... there."

"Good. Now restate that using this phrase: 'There is effortless, impersonal awareness of children talking'—removing any mention of 'I,' 'me,' or 'mine.'"

I did it, feeling slightly silly but curious about where this was going.

Then he said, "Now describe the sound to the best of your ability."

This is where it got interesting. Suddenly my mind kicked into gear. "It's my children. They're arguing about something. There's stomping, a bit of yelling. Someone's not happy about a toy or a game. They sound frustrated."

"Did it require effort to think and describe all of that?" he asked.

The difference hit me like a physical sensation. "Yes," I said, almost breathless. "Yes, it did."

"That's the difference between thought and thinking," he explained. "Thought is effortless—it just arises. Thinking requires effort. Thought comes from consciousness itself, from something beyond your personal mind. Thinking has a different quality—it's effortful, personal, analytical."

I had heard this message before. I'd read about this distinction in books, heard it in other teachings. I could have explained the concept to someone else if they'd asked.

But this time, it didn't just enter my head as information. It landed in my entire being as understanding.

In that instant, I didn't learn something intellectually—I experienced the truth behind the words. I felt the difference in my body, in my awareness, in the very fabric of how I was experiencing that moment.

From that moment on, I was a different person. I experienced the world differently. Not because I'd acquired new knowledge, but because I'd seen something that had always been true but had been invisible to me before.

That's the power of insight. It doesn't just give you new information—it gives you new eyes.

Information vs. Transformation

Let's be clear about something crucial: information lives in the intellect. Insight lives in awareness.

You can read a hundred self-help books, attend dozens of workshops, listen to countless podcasts, and still not change in any meaningful way. I know because I did exactly that for years. I was a walking encyclopedia of personal development concepts, but I was still struggling with the same patterns, the same fears, the same limitations.

But one moment of genuine insight can change everything—permanently. You don't need more answers. You need a deeper seeing.

Here's how this plays out: You might hear "You are not your thoughts" for the tenth time. The first nine times, it's just an interesting idea, something that sounds nice but doesn't really land. You nod along, maybe even repeat it to other people, but it doesn't fundamentally alter your experience.

But the tenth time—maybe you're in the middle of a thought storm, maybe you're caught in anxiety or self-criticism—suddenly something clicks. You don't just understand the concept intellectually; you feel it. You experience the truth of it in your bones.

Nothing changed externally. The words were the same. But internally? Everything shifted.

```
That's the difference between information and insight.
Information adds to what you know. Insight changes who you are.
```

The Effortless Revolution

When real insight happens, it changes you from the inside out in ways that feel almost magical:

A fear that has haunted you for years suddenly dissolves, not because you fought it but because you saw through it.

A behavioral pattern that you've been trying to break through willpower simply ends, not because you forced it to stop but because you understood something new about why it was there.

An old wound that used to sting every time you touched it no longer hurts, not because you healed it through therapy or processing but because you saw it differently.

A thought that used to have power over you loses its grip, not because you argued with it but because you recognized it for what it really was.

And here's the beautiful part: no one needs to remind you of your insight. You don't need sticky notes on your bathroom mirror or tracking apps on your phone or accountability partners to help you remember.

```
Insight self-integrates. It becomes part of your operating system.
```

It doesn't require discipline because it rewrites the code behind your behavior. When you truly see something new, you can't go back to the old way of seeing. It's like trying to believe in Santa Claus after you've discovered where the presents really come from.

I experienced this firsthand with a fear of public speaking that had plagued me since childhood. For years, I tried every technique in the book: visualization, breathing exercises, practice, exposure therapy, positive self-talk. Some of these things helped a little, but the fundamental fear remained.

Then one day, someone told me, "Ray, you're nervous about public speaking because you're focused on yourself rather than the people you are trying to help through your speaking." That hit me like a lightning bolt: I wasn't afraid of public speaking. I was afraid of being judged. And I wasn't even afraid of being judged—I was afraid of the thoughts I might have about being judged.

In that moment, I saw the whole elaborate construction of fear for what it was: a house of cards built from thoughts about thoughts about thoughts. The actual experience of speaking to a group? That was just talking to people. The fear was entirely manufactured by my own thinking.

From that day forward, public speaking stopped being a problem. Not because I conquered my fear through courage or practice, but because I saw that there was nothing real to be afraid of. The insight did all the work.

The Paradox of Trying

Here's where it gets interesting, and maybe a little frustrating: you can't force insight. You can't schedule it, manufacture it, or demand it on command.

Insight comes when the mind is quiet, not when it's trying harder.

That's why you get your best ideas in the shower, when your mind is relaxed and not focused on problem-solving.

That's why you suddenly solve a problem when you stop thinking about it and go for a walk.

That's why you sometimes forgive someone without planning to, in a moment when you're not trying to be spiritual or evolved.

The more you chase insight, the more it hides. The more you relax into presence, the more it reveals itself.

This used to drive me crazy. I wanted to be able to order insight like a pizza: "I'll take one life-changing realization, extra clarity, delivered in thirty minutes or less."

But insight doesn't work that way. It's more like a wild animal that only approaches when you're sitting very still, not trying to catch it.

I learned this lesson, where I learn many of life's most important lessons, through business struggles. One night, shortly after I had returned from my honeymoon—my head full of dreams about building a wonderful future with my new family—I logged into our business American Express account and felt my world tilt sideways.

We owed $150,000. And we had exactly one week to pay it.

My hands were shaking as I immediately called the person who managed the operations of my business. "Are we going to default on the AMEX bill?" I asked, though I already knew the answer from the sick feeling in my stomach.

The phone went silent for what seemed like five full minutes. Then, in a voice that was barely more than a whisper, he said, "Yes."

Up to this point, we had always paid the entire AMEX bill by its due date. I was shocked to discover that we were simply out of money. Here I was, ready to build a new family, and my business was on the verge of literal bankruptcy.

Now, I've always been blessed—or cursed—with a problem-solving mind.

So I did what I always do when faced with a crisis: I went into overdrive. I meditated harder, journaled more intensively, sought advice from everyone I could think of. I was like a person frantically digging for treasure, getting more and more frustrated with each empty hole.

I analyzed cash flow projections, explored loan options, considered selling assets. I made lists and charts and contingency plans. I barely slept, barely ate, my mind spinning constantly with scenarios and solutions that all seemed to lead nowhere.

Finally, after weeks of this mental torture, I was exhausted by my own efforts. I gave up. I stopped trying to figure it out. I stopped looking for the answer.

And that's when it came.

Not in meditation or journaling or deep conversation with advisors, but while I was washing dishes, my mind completely occupied with the simple, mindless task at hand. As I scrubbed a particularly stubborn pot, a question popped into my head: "Where can I get $150,000 from quickly?"

Then, in what felt like a moment of pure absurdity, my mind started fantasizing. What if I met Jeff Bezos in the supermarket and he just handed me a check for $150,000? I actually laughed out loud at the ridiculousness of it, continuing to wash dishes while mentally preparing for my next career as a dishwasher.

But then, in that moment of lightness, something struck like lightning: I will get Jeff Bezos to give me $150,000.

Not literally, of course. But suddenly I saw it—Amazon. His platform. His marketplace. The solution had been sitting there the entire time, waiting for me to stop trying so hard to find it.

I dropped the dish I was washing and went straight to my office. I immediately researched how to sell our products on Amazon.com, contacted American Express to explain our situation and arrange a payment plan, and within days had our first products listed.

Within a year, we had paid the full $150,000 with interest, all from profits made through Amazon sales. Best of all, our business was better than ever with this new revenue stream.

The answer had been so clear, so obvious, that I couldn't believe I'd been struggling with it for weeks. Amazon had been there all along—a massive, global marketplace just waiting for us to show up. But I couldn't see it while I was frantically trying to solve the problem with my thinking mind.

The insight had been there all along, waiting for me to stop trying so hard to find it.

Creating the Conditions

While you can't control insight, you can create the conditions that make it more likely to arise. Think of it like gardening—you can't force a seed to grow, but you can provide good soil, adequate water, and plenty of sunlight.

Here's how to create fertile ground for insight:

Let thought move without grabbing onto it. When your mind starts spinning, don't try to solve everything immediately. Sometimes the best thing you can do is nothing.

Respect low moods and don't try to think your way out of them. Low moods often precede insights, like the quiet before a storm. If you're constantly trying to fix your state of mind, you might miss what's trying to emerge.

Follow what feels peaceful rather than what sounds clever. Insight often comes disguised as simplicity, not complexity.

Be open to being wrong about everything you think you know. The most profound insights often contradict our existing beliefs.

Spend time in nature, in silence, in activities that don't require mental effort. Insight loves a quiet mind and an open heart.

I've noticed that my deepest insights often come when I'm doing something completely unrelated to whatever I'm trying to understand. Walking in the woods, playing with my dog, having a casual conversation with a friend— these are the moments when understanding tends to strike.

It's as if insight needs space to breathe, room to move, freedom from the pressure of our expectations.

Today's Simple Thought-Practice - Curious Stillness

Here's what I want to offer you this week—not as another technique to master, but as a way of being that invites understanding:

Instead of trying to "work on yourself," get curious.

When a pattern shows up that you don't understand, when a fear arises that seems irrational, when you find yourself stuck in a familiar struggle, try asking:

"What might I be missing here?" "What if there's a truth beneath this that I haven't seen yet?" "What if insight is already on its way?"

And then... just be still. Not the stillness of forcing your mind to be quiet, but the stillness of genuine curiosity. The stillness of someone listening for something they can't quite hear yet.

Don't try to answer the questions. Don't analyze or figure out or work through anything. Just hold the questions lightly and see what wants to emerge.

Sometimes insight comes immediately. Sometimes it takes days or weeks or months. Sometimes it comes in a form you weren't expecting, addressing something you didn't even know you were curious about.

But it always comes. Because insight isn't something you have to earn or achieve. It's something that's always available, always present, always waiting for the right moment to reveal itself.

The Only Real Change

I want to leave you with this understanding: insight is the only thing that truly changes us because it shows us what was always true.

Everything else—all the strategies and techniques and programs and methods—they might help you manage your experience or cope with your challenges. But they don't fundamentally alter who you are or how you see the world.

Insight does. In one moment of clear seeing, years of struggle can dissolve. Lifelong patterns can shift. Deep wounds can heal.

Not because you worked hard enough or tried the right approach, but because you saw something you hadn't seen before.

And once you see it, you can never unsee it.

That's the gift of insight. That's the lightning strike of understanding that illuminates everything, even in the darkness.

So this week, instead of trying to change or improve or fix anything, just get curious. Create space. Be still.

And let insight do what no amount of effort ever could: show you the truth that sets you free.

* * *

Key Insights:

- **Insight changes you because it reveals what was always true.** True transformation doesn't come from effort but from seeing something real with clarity—it's a return to what's already there beneath the noise.
- **Information is not the same as transformation.** You can accumulate knowledge without changing; transformation only happens through insight, which shifts how you see and experience reality.
- **Insight is effortless and spontaneous.** Unlike problem-solving, insight arises without effort when the mind is still—it feels like seeing the obvious for the first time.
- **Trying harder often blocks insight.** When we push and strive for answers, we tighten our thinking. But when we relax and let go, insight has space to emerge.
- **Insight self-integrates.** You don't have to "remember" insight—it becomes part of your operating system, changing you without needing reinforcement.
- **You can't force insight, but you can create space for it.** Just like you can't force a seed to grow, you can create the right conditions—quiet, openness, presence—for insight to arise naturally.

- **Insight shows up when you stop trying to fix yourself.** When we stop chasing self-improvement and get curious about our experience, we make room for deep, effortless shifts in perspective.

- **Insight often comes in ordinary moments.** It doesn't always arrive during meditation or journaling—it can hit you while doing dishes, walking the dog, or laughing at something absurd.

- **Most personal struggles are built from thought-about-thought.** Fears, patterns, and insecurities often collapse the moment we see that they're sustained by layers of overthinking, not external reality.

- **The gap between thought and thinking matters.** Effortless awareness of what is (thought) differs fundamentally from the analytical, effortful process of interpretation (thinking).

- **You already know what's true—you've just forgotten.** Insight is not about adding something new but about uncovering the truth that's been obscured by over-analysis and conditioning.

- **Low moods can precede profound breakthroughs.** Instead of fixing low states, let them be. They often clear the space for clarity to emerge when the mind finally quiets down.

- **Insight doesn't require discipline—it rewrites your code.** Once you've seen through a pattern or false belief, it loses its grip, often without the need for willpower or structured change.

- **Insight is humble and quiet—not flashy or forced.** It often arrives as a gentle whisper, not a dramatic epiphany, and it quietly reshapes your way of being from the inside out.

- **The question opens the door—the answer walks in unannounced.** Curiosity, not analysis, invites insight. Asking open questions and waiting in stillness is far more powerful than solving puzzles.

8

You Are a Self-Correcting System - Why Self-Improvement Often Backfires

"You don't need to fix your thoughts. You need to stop disturbing the clarity already there."

Y ou've probably spent years trying to fix your thoughts.
Trying to think more positively when negativity creeps in. Trying to stop the endless loop of overthinking that keeps you awake at night. Trying to control anxiety, manage mood swings, or silence those intrusive thoughts that seem to come out of nowhere.

You've read books about positive psychology, practiced mindfulness techniques, tried meditation apps, repeated affirmations, and maybe even sought therapy to help you get your mental house in order.

But what if I told you that you didn't have to fix anything?

What if your mind already knows how to settle—if you'd only let it?

In this chapter, we're going to explore something that might sound revolutionary but is actually the most natural thing in the world: the human mind is self-correcting. You don't need to fix thought—you just need to stop interfering with it.

The Natural Reset

Have you ever noticed this phenomenon? You're completely upset about something—maybe a conflict with a friend, a work situation that's stressing you out, or just one of those days when everything feels overwhelming. You're caught in the emotional storm, convinced it will never pass.

Then, thirty minutes later, you're suddenly calm. Not because you did anything special, not because you used a technique or had a breakthrough conversation. You just... settled. The storm passed on its own.

Or maybe you've experienced this: You're overthinking a decision, going around and around in mental circles, analyzing every possible angle until your brain feels like it might explode. Then, out of nowhere, clarity appears. The answer becomes obvious. The confusion lifts like morning fog.

Or this: You're spiraling about something—maybe a health concern, a relationship issue, a financial worry. Your mind is creating elaborate worst-case scenarios, and you're completely caught up in the drama. Then, a few hours later, you can barely remember what you were so worked up about.

You didn't do that. You didn't use a technique or follow a protocol or implement a strategy. It just... happened.

Because your mind, when left alone, naturally resets itself.

Think of it like a snow globe. When you shake it, the flakes swirl around in chaos, obscuring the scene inside. But if you stop shaking it and just set it down, what happens? The flakes settle. The water clears. The scene becomes visible again.

Your mind works the same way. When you stop shaking it—stop stirring up the thoughts, stop trying to control the process—it naturally returns to clarity.

Like muddy water that settles when you leave it still, your mind knows how to find its way back to peace.

The Interference Pattern

Here's what I've discovered, both in my own experience and in watching countless others struggle with their thinking: what if trying to fix your thinking is actually what keeps you stuck?

Most people approach their mental life like a mechanic working on a broken engine:

They wrestle with every thought that doesn't feel good.

They analyze every feeling, trying to understand where it came from and what it means.

They attempt to self-diagnose and optimize every state of mind, as if their consciousness were a machine that needed constant tuning.

And in doing so, they keep the system in perpetual motion.

The more you stir thought, the more it swirls. The more you grip it, the longer it sticks around. The more you try to manage it, the more chaotic it becomes.

It's like trying to calm turbulent water by stirring it with a stick. The very act of trying to fix the problem becomes the problem.

I learned this lesson the hard way during a period when I became obsessed with "optimizing" my mental state. I had discovered meditation and mindfulness, and I thought I could engineer my way to enlightenment through sheer effort and technique.

I had apps for everything: meditation timers, mood trackers, gratitude journals, breathing exercises. I monitored my thoughts like a day trader watching stock prices, constantly adjusting and correcting and trying to maintain some ideal state of consciousness. I even started referring to myself as a "biohacker" trying to hack my mind and body.

The result? I was more anxious and mentally agitated than I'd ever been in my life.

I was like someone trying to fall asleep by thinking really hard about falling asleep. The effort itself was preventing the very thing I was trying to achieve.

The mind settles when you stop treating it like a problem that needs to be solved.

The Wisdom That Emerges

You've had moments like this—I know you have, because everyone has:

You let something go that you'd been struggling with, and then a solution arises effortlessly.

You give up trying to figure something out, and peace comes flooding in.

You stop thinking about a problem, and the right action becomes crystal clear.

That's not you being lazy or giving up. That's you getting out of the way so wisdom can speak.

Wisdom isn't found through analysis. It doesn't emerge from thinking harder or trying to be smarter. It arises when the mental noise dies down, when you create space for something deeper to surface.

There is an intelligence behind life—the same intelligence that grows your hair, heals your cuts, and beats your heart without any conscious effort on your part. And that intelligence is already in you, already operating, already guiding you toward what you need to know.

You don't need to build it or develop it or earn access to it. You just need to stop overriding it with your mental management system.

I remember a time when a coaching client was struggling with what she described as depression caused by heartbreak. She had recently gone through a painful breakup, and for weeks afterward, she was caught in a spiral of sadness, self-doubt, and endless analysis about what had gone wrong.

We had a days-long text conversation about it—one of those marathon exchanges where you're trying to help someone think their way through their pain. I offered perspective, she analyzed her feelings, I suggested reframes, she explored the psychology of her patterns. Back and forth we went, diving deeper and deeper into the labyrinth of her thoughts about her thoughts about her situation.

But no progress was being made. If anything, the more we talked about it, the more entrenched she seemed to become in her suffering. It was like watching someone try to untangle a knot by pulling harder on both ends.

Finally, after what felt like hours of circular conversation, she sent me a text that stopped me in my tracks: "I just realized something. I can't think my way out of this."

The simplicity of that statement hit me like a lightning bolt. How insightful. How true. We can't think our way out of feeling. We can't solve the problem of mental suffering by using the same mental processes that created it.

Her insight became my insight in that moment. I realized I had been trying to think my way into feeling more successful, more confident, more at peace. I had been using my mind to try to fix my mind, like trying to lift yourself up by pulling on your own shoelaces.

It doesn't work. It can't work. The very effort keeps you stuck in the same loop you're trying to escape.

Within a few days of her realization, something shifted for my client. Not because she had figured anything out or solved her heartbreak through analysis, but because she had stopped trying to. She had given up the exhausting job of managing her emotional experience and allowed her natural resilience to emerge.

The depression didn't disappear overnight, but it began to move and change in ways that felt organic rather than forced. She started to have moments of lightness, glimpses of her old self, periods where she forgot to be sad because she was engaged with life again.

The wisdom had been there all along, waiting patiently for her to stop drowning it out with mental noise.

The Passenger, Not the Engineer

Here's a metaphor that changed everything for me: Imagine if you had to consciously beat your heart, regulate your hormones, digest your food, and manage your immune system. You'd be exhausted within minutes. You'd never have time or energy for anything else.

Yet your body knows exactly what to do. It has an intelligence that operates far beyond your conscious control, managing thousands of complex processes every second without any input from your thinking mind.

Your mental and emotional life works the same way.

You're not the engineer of your inner experience. You're not supposed to be managing every thought, controlling every feeling, or optimizing every state of consciousness.

You're the awareness that observes it all—the passenger riding the waves, not the one trying to control the ocean.

When you trust the system, you give up the exhausting job of trying to control everything, and you gain something far more valuable: clarity, peace. The ability to respond from wisdom rather than react from mental noise.

This doesn't mean you become passive or indifferent. It means you stop interfering with a process that already knows how to work perfectly.

The Art of Non-Interference

So what does this look like practically? How do you stop fixing and start trusting?

This week, I want to invite you to experiment with something radical: letting go of the need to manage your mental experience.

When a difficult thought arises—when anxiety shows up, when self-doubt creeps in, when your mind starts spinning with worry—try this:

Don't reframe it into something more positive.

Don't try to control it or make it go away.

Don't fight it or argue with it or analyze where it came from.

Just notice it. Give it space. And wait.

I know this might sound too simple, maybe even irresponsible. We've been taught that we need to actively manage our mental health, that we're supposed to challenge negative thoughts and replace them with positive ones.

But what if that's exactly backwards? What if the very act of trying to manage our thoughts is what keeps them stuck in place?

Think about it: when you try to push away a thought, what happens? It pushes back. When you fight with anxiety, it fights back harder. When you try to force yourself to feel better, you often end up feeling worse.

But when you simply notice what's happening without trying to change it, something interesting occurs. The thought or feeling doesn't have anything to push against. It's like trying to have an argument with someone who just nods and says, "Interesting."

Without resistance, thoughts naturally move. They arise, they're acknowledged, and they pass on their own.

The Experiment

Here's a simple experiment you can try right now:

Think of something that's been bothering you lately—nothing too intense, just something that's been on your mind. Maybe it's a work situation, a relationship concern, or just a general worry about the future.

Now, instead of trying to solve it or think your way through it, just sit with it for a moment. Don't try to make it go away, but don't feed it either. Just let it be there, like a cloud passing through the sky of your awareness.

Notice what happens. Does the thought change on its own? Does it lose some of its emotional charge? Does it reveal something you hadn't seen before?

You might be surprised how often thought moves and shifts and settles when you stop trying to control it.

The Deeper Trust

What I'm really talking about here is a fundamental shift in how you relate to your own mind. Instead of seeing yourself as the manager of your mental experience, you start to see yourself as the space in which all experience occurs.

You are not a project to fix. You are not a mess to manage. You are not your thought content.

You are the quiet awareness that already contains wisdom, that already knows how to navigate life, that already has access to everything you need.

This awareness doesn't need to be improved or optimized or managed. It just needs to be trusted.

When you trust the system—when you step back and allow your natural intelligence to operate—you discover something remarkable: your mind really does know how to settle. Your emotions really do know how to flow and change. Your wisdom really is always available.

Not because you've learned the right techniques or followed the right program, but because that's simply how the system is designed to work.

Today's Simple Thought-Practice

So here's my invitation to you: for the next week, practice being a passenger instead of a driver. When your mind gets busy, instead of trying to calm it down, just observe it with curiosity. When difficult emotions arise, instead of trying to fix them, just give them space to be there.

See what happens when you stop disturbing the clarity that's already there.

You might discover that the peace you've been seeking, the wisdom you've been trying to develop, the clarity you've been working toward—it's all already present, just waiting for you to stop interfering with it.

Because the truth is, you don't need to fix your thoughts. You just need to stop shaking the snow globe and let the natural clarity of your mind reveal itself.

Trust the system. It knows what it's doing.

$$* * *$$

Key Insights:

- **You don't need to fix your thoughts—just stop disturbing the clarity that's already there.** The mind is naturally self-correcting, like a snow globe that clears when left alone. The more you interfere, the more you stir up chaos.
- **The mind resets itself when left alone.** Just like muddy water settles when still, your mental state calms and clarifies when you stop trying to fix or manage it.

- **Trying to fix thought often sustains the problem.** When we constantly analyze, reframe, or battle our thoughts, we energize and prolong them instead of letting them pass.
- **Interference blocks wisdom.** Wisdom and clarity arise not from mental effort but from stillness. When we quiet down, answers emerge naturally.
- **Over-managing your mental state backfires.** Tracking, optimizing, and analyzing every mood often creates more agitation than peace. Peace arises when you stop efforting.
- **Insight can't be engineered through thinking.** You can't think your way out of thinking. Insight comes when you drop the need to solve and simply become present.
- **You're not the engineer of your inner life.** Just like you don't control your heartbeat, you don't need to control every thought. Your system works best when trusted.
- **Mental peace isn't created—it's revealed.** Peace is the default state of a quiet mind. It's not something you manufacture—it's what remains when you stop disturbing.
- **Resistance fuels persistence.** When you fight thoughts, they fight back. Non-resistance allows them to move on their own without drama or control.
- **You are awareness, not the thoughts passing through it.** Thoughts are transient. The real "you" is the quiet background—capable of observing without getting entangled.
- **Clarity emerges in stillness, not struggle.** Many breakthroughs happen in relaxed moments—like walking, showering, or doing nothing— because insight needs space.
- **Wisdom is always available.** You don't earn or build wisdom—it's already part of you. It just gets drowned out by mental noise and overthinking.
- **Letting go makes space for natural healing.** When you stop managing pain or distress, your inner resilience kicks in. Healing begins the moment interference ends.
- **Simplicity is not irresponsibility.** Giving thought space doesn't mean passivity—it's a radical trust in the system to do what it's designed to do.

· **Trusting the system leads to true peace.** When you stop trying to control your mind and instead let it be, you access the deep calm, clarity, and intelligence that was always there.

9

The Secret to 24/7 Personal Peace

"Peace isn't something you get. It's what's left when you stop chasing thought."

When most people seek peace of mind, they approach it like a destination they need to reach. They meditate harder, trying to force their minds into submission. They eliminate distractions from their environment, believing that external quiet will create internal stillness. They chase peace through breath work, mantras, visualization techniques, and endless spiritual practices.

They treat a quiet mind like a goal to achieve, a skill to develop, a state to earn through effort and discipline.

But here's the radical truth that changes everything: You don't need to get to a quiet mind. That's where you started.

Peace isn't something you create or accomplish or work toward. It's what you are, underneath all the mental noise. It's your default setting, your factory original, your true nature that's been there all along, waiting patiently for you to stop looking everywhere else for it.

What's Left When the Dust Settles

Your natural state isn't stress, anxiety, or endless thinking loops. Those are just weather patterns passing through the sky of your consciousness.

Your natural state is presence. Awareness. Quiet.

You've touched this state many times, probably more often than you realize:

In those moments of awe watching a sunset, when time seems to stop and you forget to think about anything at all.

Watching a baby sleep, when something in their perfect peace reminds you of your own.

Getting completely lost in music or nature, when the boundary between you and the world dissolves.

After a deep insight, when understanding lands and your mind goes completely still.

In those moments, thought drops away. And what's left?

You. The real you. Quiet, whole, and aware.

Not a you that you created through effort or technique, but the you that was always there, temporarily obscured by mental activity but never actually damaged or lost.

I remember the first time I really noticed this. I was sitting by a lake early one morning, not meditating or trying to be spiritual, just drinking coffee and watching the water. The surface was perfectly still, reflecting the sky like a mirror.

As I sat there, I realized that my mind had become just as still as the water. I wasn't thinking about my to-do list or my problems or my plans for the day. I wasn't trying not to think about them—they just weren't there.

In that stillness, I felt more like myself than I had in months. Not a better version of myself or an improved version, but more authentically, simply myself. It was like taking off shoes that had been too tight and feeling the relief of being natural again.

That's when I understood: this peace wasn't something I had achieved. It was something I had returned to.

The Art of Not Stirring

Here's what I've learned about stillness: you don't create it—you return to it.

Stillness doesn't come from doing more meditation, reading more spiritual books, or perfecting your mindfulness practice. It comes from letting go of the effort to be somewhere other than where you are.

Trying to force a quiet mind is like yelling at ocean waves to stop crashing. You can stand on the beach and shout all you want, but the waves will keep doing what waves do. But if you watch patiently, if you stop trying to control the ocean, you'll notice something beautiful: the waves always settle on their own. Between each wave is a moment of perfect stillness.

Your mind works the same way. It's like a pond that becomes muddy when you stir it but clears naturally when you leave it alone. The clarity isn't something you add to the water—it's what's revealed when you stop disturbing it.

So don't chase stillness. Don't grip your mind tighter, trying to squeeze peace out of it like water from a stone. Instead, relax into the space that's already here, the awareness that's already present, the peace that's already your nature.

This was a hard lesson for me to learn because I'm naturally someone who likes to fix things, to work on problems, to make improvements through effort. When I first discovered meditation and mindfulness, I approached them like any other skill I wanted to develop. I set goals, tracked my progress, tried to get better at being peaceful.

The result was that I became very good at meditating but not very good at being at peace. I could sit still for half-an-hour and follow my breath and observe my thoughts, but the moment I opened my eyes, I was right back in the mental noise I'd been trying to escape.

It wasn't until I stopped trying to achieve peace and started noticing the peace that was already there that everything shifted. I realized I'd been like someone searching frantically for their glasses while wearing them.

Meditation Without the Manual

You don't need a script to be still. You don't need perfect posture, meditation timers, or elaborate techniques. You don't need to sit in a specific position or breathe in a particular way or repeat certain words.

All you need to do is notice what's already present when you're not chasing thought.

Here's the simplest practice I know:

Sit somewhere comfortable. Breathe normally. Don't try to control your breath or make it deeper or slower—just let it be whatever it is.

When thoughts arise—and they will—don't engage with them. Don't fight them or try to push them away, but don't follow them either. Let them come and go like clouds passing through the sky.

You're not trying to stop thinking. You're just not participating in the thinking. You're being the sky, not the clouds.

That's it. No mantras, no visualizations, no complex instructions. Just the simple recognition that you are the awareness in which all experience occurs, and that awareness is naturally peaceful.

You'll notice something remarkable: stillness was never far away. You were just busy looking elsewhere for it.

Why This Matters

When your mind naturally quiets—not through force but through understanding—something beautiful happens:

You hear wisdom more clearly because there's less mental noise drowning it out.

You feel grounded, even during chaos, because you're connected to some-thing deeper than circumstances.

You make decisions from insight rather than panic because you're not caught up in the emotional storm.

You feel more loving, relaxed, and authentically yourself because you're not trying to be anyone else.

But here's the key: you don't need to strive for these benefits. You don't need to earn them or work toward them or prove you deserve them.

You just need to see that this peaceful awareness is already your nature. Like a snow globe, you don't build the stillness—you just let the flurry of thoughts pass and watch as clarity naturally emerges.

A friend once told me a story that perfectly captures this understanding. She was talking to a father who described a moment with his five-year-old daughter. The little girl had been upset about something—he couldn't even remember what—and she was crying and carrying on. He was trying to comfort her, offering solutions and distractions, when she suddenly stopped mid-sob and announced, "Daddy, I'm not sad anymore."

"What happened?" he asked, genuinely curious. "How did you stop being sad?"

She looked at him with that matter-of-fact wisdom that children sometimes have and said, "I just remembered I'm not a sad person."

In that moment, this little girl had touched something profound. She had recognized that her essential nature—her true self—wasn't defined by the temporary emotional weather passing through her experience. She was the sky, not the storm.

That's what happens when we remember our true nature. We don't become peaceful—we remember that we are peace, temporarily obscured by mental activity but never actually lost.

The Deepest Rest

There's a quality of rest that comes from this understanding that's different from any other kind of relaxation. It's not the rest of sleep or vacation or even meditation. It's the rest of coming home to yourself.

It's the rest of no longer trying to be someone else, no longer working to improve yourself, no longer chasing states of consciousness or spiritual experiences.

It's the rest of recognizing that what you've been seeking has been here all along, closer than your own breath, more intimate than your own thoughts.

This rest is available to you right now, not as something you need to achieve but as something you can simply notice. It's the stillness between thoughts, the space between breaths, the awareness that remains constant while everything else changes.

The Invitation

So let this truth land gently in your understanding: You are not here to achieve a peaceful mind. You already have one. It's just been covered up by the belief that you need to get somewhere else, be someone else, or accomplish something more to be worthy of peace.

There's nothing to chase, nothing to fix, nothing to earn.

Stillness isn't the reward for good spiritual practice—it's the reminder of who you've always been.

Peace isn't something you get—it's what's left when you stop chasing thought.

This week, instead of trying to meditate your way to peace, just notice the peace that's already here. Instead of working to quiet your mind, just observe the quiet that exists in the spaces between thoughts.

You might be surprised to discover that what you've been seeking through so much effort and striving has been patiently waiting for you to simply turn around and see it.

Like Dorothy in the Wizard of Oz, you've always had the power to go home. You just had to learn that home was never a place you needed to travel to—it was what you are.

* * *

Key Insights:

- **Peace isn't something you get—it's what's left when thought quiets.** Peace isn't earned or created; it's your natural state, revealed when you stop chasing, fixing, or managing your thoughts.
- **Stillness is your original setting.** You began life in peace. The stress and noise are overlays—like dust on a mirror—not who or what you truly are.
- **You've already experienced true peace.** In moments of awe, beauty, or deep presence, thought drops away—and what's left is you, undisturbed and whole.
- **The mind quiets when left alone.** Just like a stirred pond settles on its own, your mind becomes still when you stop disturbing it with effort and fixing.
- **You can't force peace—you return to it.** Trying to "achieve" stillness creates more agitation. Real peace comes from letting go, not gripping harder.
- **Stillness doesn't need techniques.** You don't need mantras, apps, or perfect posture. Peace is already there—it's the background of awareness.
- **You're the sky, not the storm.** Thoughts, feelings, and moods are like weather passing through. You remain the constant sky—open, quiet, and clear.
- **Effort often prevents the very peace we seek.** When you strive for mental stillness, you create tension. Peace arises when striving ends.
- **Wisdom surfaces in the absence of noise.** When mental chatter fades, clarity and insight emerge effortlessly—like the answer arriving after you stop searching.
- **Real meditation is non-participation.** You don't stop thoughts—you simply stop following them. Like watching clouds drift by without chasing or judging.
- **Peace is found in being, not doing.** It's not something you accomplish—it's something you notice when you stop trying to be different or better.
- **Children often embody this truth.** Like the little girl who remembered she wasn't a sad person, we too can recall we are not our emotions or

mental states.

- **The deepest rest comes from returning to yourself.** Not from sleep or relaxation, but from no longer needing to be anything other than what you already are.
- **There's nothing to fix, earn, or chase.** Stillness is not a prize for effort— it's the space always available beneath the layers of striving.
- **Home was never far—it's what you are.** Like Dorothy's journey in Oz, the peace you're searching for isn't out there. It's been with you the whole time.

10

Why You Will Fail and Why That's Not a Problem

"Even when the sky goes dark, the sun is still there."

Y ou know the teachings. You understand how experience works from the inside-out. You've seen the nature of thought, recognized that you're not your thinking, maybe even had some profound insights that shifted everything.

You've felt that beautiful clarity, that sense of peace, that knowing that you are so much more than the stories in your head.

But then, out of nowhere, it happens.

You're anxious again. Spiraling in self-doubt. Caught in a familiar loop of worry or frustration or fear. Back in the mental storm you thought you'd left behind.

And immediately, the thoughts start:

"Did I lose it?" "Did I mess up somehow?" "Why am I back here again?" "Maybe I didn't really get it after all." "I thought I was past this."

Let me offer you the most reassuring truth I know: You're not off track. You're not broken. You haven't lost anything. You're just in thought.

And that's completely, utterly, beautifully normal.

The Weather Report

Let's clear something up right from the start: getting caught in thought doesn't mean you're broken. Feeling low doesn't mean you're back at square one. Overthinking doesn't mean you've failed to understand the principles or that you're a bad student of this understanding.

It just means you're human.

Even Sydney Banks, the man who first articulated these principles after his profound awakening, had moods. He had days when his thinking got busy, moments when he felt less clear, times when the mental weather was stormy.

The difference wasn't that he never experienced thought storms—it's that he understood what they were. He knew they were temporary weather patterns, not permanent features of his landscape.

That understanding didn't erase the storms. It stopped him from believing they meant something was wrong with him.

Think about it this way: when clouds cover the sun, do you panic that the sun has disappeared forever? When your phone loses signal, do you assume the entire internet has been destroyed? When a wave knocks you over at the beach, do you conclude that you're no longer capable of swimming?

Of course not. You understand that these are temporary conditions that don't change the fundamental reality underneath.

The same is true for thought storms. They're temporary weather in the sky of your consciousness. They don't mean you've lost your understanding or that you're back where you started. They just mean you're temporarily caught up in the weather.

The Illusion of Going Backwards

Here's something I see all the time: people who have had genuine insights, who really understand these principles, get caught in a thought storm and immediately conclude they've regressed. They think they've lost their understanding, that they're back to being the anxious, confused person they were before.

But that's not how understanding works. Just because you're caught in thinking doesn't mean your insight is gone.

Imagine you're an experienced driver who's been driving for years. One day, you get distracted and take a wrong turn. Does that mean you've forgotten how to drive? Does it erase all your years of experience behind the wheel?

Of course not. You're still a driver who temporarily got off course. You still know how to drive—you just need to remember where you're going and get back on track.

The experience of being lost in thought is temporary noise, not proof that your wisdom has vanished. You haven't regressed. You've just forgotten temporarily. And the system—your natural intelligence, your innate wisdom—will remind you again.

I remember a period when I was going through some business challenges, and I found myself caught in weeks of anxious thinking. I was worried about money, stressed about decisions I needed to make, spinning in mental loops about worst-case scenarios.

Part of me was frustrated with myself. "I know better than this," I thought. "I understand how thought works. Why am I still getting caught up in this stuff?"

But then I realized: the very fact that I could see I was caught up in thinking was proof that my understanding was still intact. The awareness that could observe the thought storm was the same awareness that had always been there. I hadn't lost anything—I was just temporarily identified with the weather instead of remembering I was the sky.

The Setup for Clarity

Here's something beautiful and paradoxical: sometimes the very moment you realize "Oh wow, I'm deep in thought right now" becomes an insight in itself.

That moment of recognition—that "aha" when you see you've been caught up in mental drama—is actually a return to clarity. It's like waking up from a dream and realizing you were dreaming.

In that moment, the game shifts. Not because you controlled the storm or made it go away through effort, but because you remembered what's true. You remembered that you are not the storm—you are the awareness in which storms arise and pass away.

Sometimes, getting completely caught up in thinking is the perfect setup for a deeper realization. It's like the contrast that makes you appreciate the light. The darker the night, the more brilliant the dawn appears.

I've noticed this pattern in my own life and in the lives of others: often our deepest insights come right after our most intense thought storms. It's as if we need to get completely lost to remember how to find our way home.

A thought storm isn't a setback—it's a setup for clarity.

The Gentle Way Through

So what actually helps when you find yourself caught in a mental tempest? What's the most effective way to navigate these inevitable storms?

Not self-blame. Beating yourself up for being human just adds more turbulence to the system.

Not analysis. Trying to figure out why you're thinking what you're thinking just creates more thinking.

Not panic. Getting urgent about fixing your state of mind just creates more urgency.

The most helpful response is compassion. Gentle, patient, loving compassion for yourself as a human being having a human experience.

"Ah... this is one of those moments. I forgot who I really am for a while."

"That's okay. I'll remember again. I always do."

"No need to fix anything or figure anything out. I'll just ride this one out."

"This too shall pass."

This is how a thought storm becomes less sticky: you don't feed it with shame, urgency, or the need to make it go away. You just let it be what it is—weather passing through.

I think of it like being caught in a rainstorm. You can stand there shaking your fist at the sky, demanding that the rain stop immediately. You can analyze why it's raining and try to understand the meteorological conditions that created the storm. You can panic about getting wet and run around frantically looking for shelter.

Or you can simply acknowledge that it's raining, maybe find an umbrella or a doorway to wait it out, and trust that all storms eventually pass.

The rain doesn't care about your analysis or your urgency. But your experience of being in the rain changes dramatically depending on how you relate to it.

The Deeper Knowing

Here's what I want you to remember the next time you find yourself in a thought storm: underneath all the mental weather, there's a part of you that knows. A part that remembers. A part that remains untouched by the temporary turbulence.

That part of you—your essential self, your true nature, your deepest wisdom—doesn't come and go. It doesn't get stronger or weaker based on your mood or your circumstances or how much thinking is happening.

It's like the sun behind the clouds. Even when you can't see it, even when the sky is completely overcast, the sun is still there, still shining, still constant.

Your peace, your wisdom, your fundamental okayness—these aren't achievements you can lose or skills you can forget. They're what you are, temporarily obscured by mental activity but never actually damaged or diminished.

The Invitation to Trust

So the next time you feel lost, off track, or caught in a familiar pattern of thinking, I invite you to remember this:

You didn't lose anything. You didn't go backwards. You're not broken or failing or doing this wrong.

You're just temporarily caught in the illusion again. And you'll remember your way out, just like you always have.

Because you already know the truth underneath all the mental noise. You've touched it, felt it, lived from it. That knowing doesn't disappear just because clouds pass over it.

The storm will pass. It always does. And when it does, you'll find yourself exactly where you've always been: home, in the quiet center of your own being, wondering why you ever thought you could be anywhere else.

Even when the sky goes dark, the sun is still there. And so are you—whole, perfect, and free, just temporarily forgetting to look up.

* * *

Key Insights:

- **You haven't lost your clarity—you're just in a thought storm.** When anxiety, self-doubt, or frustration return, it doesn't mean you've gone backward. It means you're caught in temporary thinking, not that your understanding is gone.
- **Getting caught in thought is normal.** Even enlightened teachers have mental weather. Feeling off or anxious doesn't mean you're broken—just human.
- **You're not your mental weather—you're the sky.** Thoughts and moods are like clouds. They pass. The sky—your awareness—remains untouched.
- **Insight doesn't vanish just because clarity fades.** Like a seasoned driver who takes a wrong turn, your wisdom is still there, even if you're momentarily off course.
- **Recognition of confusion is a return to clarity.** Realizing you're caught in thought is itself an awakening. That moment of awareness marks the shift back to presence.
- **Thought storms often precede breakthroughs.** Periods of intense mental activity often lead to powerful insight. The storm sets up the stillness that follows.

- **Self-blame adds turbulence to the system.** Judging yourself for being "off" only creates more thinking. Compassion softens the experience and helps you return to center.
- **You can't think your way out of a thought storm.** Analyzing your feelings or trying to fix your mood with thought only deepens the loop.
- **Compassion is the gentlest path through mental storms.** Meeting yourself with kindness and patience lets the storm pass naturally, without resistance.
- **The storm isn't the problem—your reaction is.** Panicking, fixing, or overanalyzing creates friction. Calm acceptance lets thought settle on its own.
- **The deeper you is always untouched.** No matter how turbulent your surface thoughts, your essential self—peaceful and wise—is still shining beneath.
- **Understanding doesn't prevent storms—it transforms your relationship to them.** The goal isn't to never have thought storms but to see them clearly and not take them so seriously.
- **Wisdom doesn't depend on your mood.** You don't lose wisdom when your mind is noisy—it's simply harder to hear. But it's still there, always.
- **Your state of mind isn't proof of progress or failure.** Low moods don't mean you've regressed. They're part of the ebb and flow of thought—not indicators of truth.
- **You're always one thought away from remembering who you are.** The shift doesn't require effort. Just one moment of awareness is enough to return home.

11

Should I Give Up Self-Help? Understanding The Map and the Territory

"Methods are maps. The Thought Principle explains the terrain."

You might be wondering: Can I still meditate? Can I use breathwork? What about therapy, journaling, or other healing modalities I've found helpful? Does embracing the Thought Principle mean I have to toss out everything else I've learned about personal growth and healing?

It's a fair question, and one I hear often from people who've discovered this understanding but don't want to abandon practices that have served them well.

Let me offer you a simple but profound answer: The Thought Principle isn't in competition with other approaches. It's the operating system beneath all approaches.

Understanding this distinction changes everything—not just about how you view other modalities, but about how you use them, relate to them, and ultimately, how much you need them at all.

The Description, Not the Prescription

Here's the first thing to understand: The Thought Principle doesn't tell you what to do. It explains what is already happening.

It is a description of how all human experience is created—from the inside-out—through thought. It's not a method or technique or practice. It's more like the laws of physics for psychological experience.

Think of it this way: gravity doesn't tell you how to walk, but it explains why you don't float away when you take a step. The Thought Principle doesn't tell you how to heal or grow or find peace, but it explains how all healing, growth, and peace actually occur.

So no matter what method you use—meditation, therapy, breathwork, journaling, yoga, energy work, cognitive behavioral therapy—it only works through the same fundamental principle: thought creates experience. There's no other way for human experience to be created.

This understanding doesn't invalidate other approaches. If anything, it illuminates why they work when they do work, and why they sometimes don't.

How Techniques Actually Work

Let's say you use meditation to relax, journaling to gain insight, breathwork to manage anxiety, or cognitive therapy to shift your thinking patterns.

Here's what's actually happening: None of these techniques cause peace, insight, or healing directly. What they do is create conditions for your natural wisdom and well-being to be noticed.

They may distract you from stressful thinking temporarily. They might quiet your mental chatter for a while. They could interrupt your habitual thought patterns and give you a fresh perspective.

But the healing, the insight, the peace—that never comes from the technique itself. It comes from the clarity that arises when thought settles, when you connect with something deeper than your thinking mind, when you remember who you really are underneath all the mental noise.

I learned this lesson during a period when I was heavily invested in various personal development practices. I had a morning routine that included meditation, journaling, breathwork, and affirmations. I tracked my mood, monitored my thoughts, and worked diligently on "improving" myself.

Some days, the practices seemed to work beautifully. I'd feel peaceful after meditation, gain clarity through journaling, feel energized after breathwork. Other days, I'd go through the exact same routine and feel nothing—or sometimes even worse than when I started.

I couldn't understand why the techniques were so inconsistent. If they were truly effective, shouldn't they work every time?

Then I began to understand the Thought Principle, and everything made sense. The techniques weren't creating the peace or clarity—they were simply creating space for me to notice the peace and clarity that were already there. On the days when I felt good after my practices, it wasn't because the practices had manufactured those feelings. It was because my thinking had settled enough for my natural well-being to shine through.

On the days when the practices didn't "work," it was usually because I was trying too hard, expecting too much, or caught up in thinking about whether I was doing them right.

The Light Touch

So should you throw away all your other tools and practices? Not necessarily. But here's the shift that changes everything:

```
Use them with understanding, not dependency.
```

Don't give the power to the breathwork, the mantra, the therapy session, or the healing modality. See them as optional doorways, not essential crutches.

When you understand the principle underlying all experience, you'll find that:

You need fewer tools because you're not trying to fix something that was never broken.

You use the tools you do choose more lightly because you're not desperate for them to work.

You're less identified with needing specific results because you know that your well-being doesn't depend on any particular outcome.

This doesn't mean you become indifferent or stop caring about growth and healing. It means you stop making your peace conditional on external methods working perfectly.

I still meditate sometimes, but not because I need to quiet my mind. I meditate because I enjoy the simplicity of sitting quietly, and I know that my mind will quiet itself when it's ready.

I still journal occasionally, but not because I need to process my emotions or figure out my life. I journal because sometimes it's pleasant to let thoughts flow onto paper, and I trust that any insights I need will arise naturally.

I still work with coaches when it feels right, but not because I'm broken and need fixing. I work with them because I enjoy the conversation, the different perspectives, the opportunity to explore ideas with someone skilled in listening.

The difference is in the relationship to these practices. They've become preferences rather than necessities, choices rather than compulsions.

The Ultimate Freedom

Here's what I've noticed: the more deeply someone understands the Thought Principle, the less they tend to rely on external tools and techniques. Not from discipline or willpower, but from insight.

You simply stop needing to manage or control your mind because you understand how it actually works.

You don't meditate to quiet your mind—you realize the mind quiets itself when you stop stirring it up.

You don't do therapy to fix your past—you realize the past only exists in present-moment thinking.

You don't use breathwork to manage anxiety—you see that anxiety is created by anxious thinking, and thinking is temporary.

This isn't about becoming anti-technique or dismissing the value of various healing modalities. Many of these approaches can be beautiful, helpful, and even transformative. It's about understanding what's actually happening when they work, and not making your well-being dependent on them.

The Integration

So can you combine the Thought Principle with other approaches? Absolutely—if you do it from clarity rather than confusion.

The key is to see what's always true underneath every modality: that all experience is created from the inside-out through thought. When you see this clearly, you'll never be bound by any particular method again.

You might still choose to use various techniques, but you'll use them as someone who understands the territory, not someone who's lost and desperately following any map they can find.

You'll approach healing and growth from a place of wholeness rather than brokenness, curiosity rather than urgency, trust rather than fear.

And paradoxically, when you stop needing techniques to work, they often work better. When you stop being desperate for healing, healing happens more naturally. When you stop trying so hard to grow, growth becomes effortless.

The Deeper Understanding

What I want to leave you with is this: techniques are helpful, but insight is transformational. Understanding changes everything—even how you heal.

When you really see how experience is created, when you understand that you are not broken and never were, when you recognize that peace and wisdom are your natural state rather than achievements to be earned, everything shifts.

You might still use various tools and practices, but you'll use them as someone who knows they're already whole, already wise, already free. And that changes everything about how those tools work and what they can offer you.

The Thought Principle doesn't replace other modalities—it reveals what's been true all along underneath every effective approach to healing and growth. It shows you the territory that all the maps have been trying to help you navigate.

And once you know the territory intimately, you realize you never needed the maps as much as you thought you did. You were always capable of finding your way home.

* * *

Key Insights:

- **The Thought Principle describes how experience works, not what to do.** It's not a technique or strategy—it's the underlying mechanism of all experience, much like gravity explains motion without prescribing movement.
- **Healing and growth don't come from methods—they come through insight.** Techniques may quiet thought or distract from it, but real peace arises when thought settles on its own and deeper awareness emerges.
- **All methods work (when they do) via the same mechanism: the settling of thought.** Whether it's breathwork, meditation, or therapy—if it helps, it's because it temporarily quiets your thinking, not because it contains healing power.
- **Understanding how experience is created frees you from needing techniques.** You realize peace isn't something you generate through tools—it's what's uncovered when you stop interfering with your natural state.
- **You don't need to abandon tools—you just stop depending on them.** You can still enjoy your favorite practices, but with a light touch instead of clinging to them as if they're essential for peace.
- **The real power is in seeing—not in doing.** Insight into how thought

creates feeling brings a deeper transformation than any behavioral or emotional hack ever could.

- **Using methods without understanding breeds dependency.** When you believe the technique is the source of peace, you chase practices rather than trusting your own inner intelligence.
- **Techniques can become gentle doorways—not crutches.** With insight, you use practices like journaling or meditation not to fix yourself, but to gently reflect what's already true beneath the noise.
- **When you stop needing peace to show up, it often does.** Non-attachment to results actually opens the door for the natural clarity and wisdom that techniques aim to reveal.
- **The Thought Principle is compatible with other modalities—if seen clearly.** You can still blend this understanding with therapy, coaching, or spiritual practices—so long as you recognize where the experience is truly coming from.
- **Less effort, more trust.** You stop trying to manufacture peace and begin trusting that your system already knows how to return to balance.
- **True change doesn't require techniques—it requires seeing what's already true.** You don't have to earn clarity. When you stop believing the illusion, clarity is what's left.
- **You begin using practices for enjoyment, not salvation.**
- You journal because it feels expressive, not because you're trying to solve your life. You meditate because you enjoy quiet, not because you need to be fixed.
- **Insight makes techniques work better—or unnecessary.** Ironically, when you no longer depend on practices, they become more enjoyable— and sometimes irrelevant altogether.
- **The real transformation is realizing you were never broken.** The Thought Principle reveals that peace, wisdom, and clarity were always your baseline—methods just helped you notice what was already there.

12

Thought & Relationships – You're Not Reacting to People. You're Reacting to Thought.

"You don't react to others. You react to the meaning your thoughts assign to them."

Let's talk about relationships—partners, parents, friends, co-workers, that person who cut you off in traffic this morning.

Most of us believe that our experience of others is caused by what they say, what they do, how they treat us. We think our emotional reactions are direct responses to their behavior, their words, their actions.

But here's a truth that can completely transform how you relate to everyone in your life:

```
You are never reacting to people. You are always reacting to your
thinking about people.
```

This one shift—this simple recognition of where your experience is actually coming from—can revolutionize every relationship you have.

The Invisible Filter

You never interact with someone directly. You interact with your perception of them, filtered through the lens of your own thinking.

Here's how it works:

They speak → You interpret what they mean.

They act → You assign intention and significance.

They send a text → You fill in tone, emotion, and backstory.

In other words, it's not what they did—it's what you think it means.

This explains why the same person can feel completely different to you from one day to the next, or even from one moment to the next. Your partner's silence can feel peaceful and comfortable one day, threatening and cold the next. Your child's outburst can seem amusing and age-appropriate in one moment, disrespectful and infuriating in another. A simple "Hey" in a text message can be read as loving and warm or distant and dismissive.

The person didn't change. Their behavior might have been identical. But your thinking about them, your interpretation of their actions, your story about what it all means—that's what created your entirely different experience.

I witnessed this phenomenon firsthand with a friend, who is very active on LinkedIn. One day, a colleague she works closely with—someone she considered both a friend and confidant—blocked her out of the blue on the platform.

She took immediate offense and quickly concocted an elaborate story about why this had happened and what it meant. The blocking wasn't just a simple action—in her mind, it became evidence of betrayal, corporate politics, professional jealousy, or some other sinister motivation.

During a conversation, I found myself in the familiar position of trying to explain the Thought Principle to someone who knows me too well to take my wisdom seriously. As they say, "A prophet is accepted everywhere but in their homeland."

I was simply trying to convey that what was factually true was that she appeared to be blocked from her colleague's profile. Everything else—all the meaning, all the interpretation, all the dramatic backstory—was just thought. Stories her mind was creating to explain a simple digital action.

"You can't possibly know why you were blocked," I said. "It could be anything. Maybe it was an accident. Maybe they're having technical issues. Maybe they're taking a social media break. Maybe they're secretly looking for a new job and don't want others in the company to know. Maybe they accidentally hit the wrong button."

She wasn't buying it. She was convinced that the only reasonable explanation was that her colleague was deliberately distancing herself, probably due to some complex web of corporate politics or professional rivalry that she was now mentally mapping out in vivid detail.

A few days later, her colleague unblocked her, and all was well. They had a brief conversation, and it turned out the reason was perfectly harmless and explainable—nothing diabolical.

My friend didn't have to do anything. She didn't need to confront anyone, defend herself, or navigate any complex political situation. The entire drama had existed only in her thinking about what the blocking meant, not in any actual relationship conflict.

The entire emotional roller coaster—the hurt, the anger, the sense of betrayal, the strategic planning about how to handle the "situation"—all of it was created by her thoughts about a simple technical action, not by the action itself.

When Thought Systems Collide

Ever been in a heated argument with someone, only to realize hours or days later that it was essentially about nothing? That what felt like a major conflict in the moment seems almost silly in retrospect?

That's because most relationship conflicts aren't caused by events or circumstances. They're caused by clashing narratives—your story about what happened colliding with their story about what happened. It's thought, just thought.

You believe they disrespected you. They believe you're being controlling.

You think they're not listening. They think you're being unreasonable. You feel unappreciated. They feel criticized.

Neither perspective is "the truth"—both are thought-created interpretations of whatever actually occurred.

Two thought systems collide, and we mistake it for "relationship drama." We think we're arguing about who's right or what really happened, but we're actually just defending our respective stories about what it all means.

Consider this scenario: Someone has an intense argument with a friend about something the friend said during a group conversation. They become convinced that the friend deliberately undermined them in front of others, making a comment that felt dismissive and condescending. They feel hurt and angry, and they express this.

The friend is genuinely confused by this reaction. From their perspective, they had been making a lighthearted joke, the kind of playful banter they'd always engaged in. They had no intention of undermining anyone and couldn't understand why it was being taken so seriously.

They go back and forth, each trying to convince the other of their version of reality. One insists that the comment was inappropriate and hurtful. The other insists that the first person is being overly sensitive and misinterpreting their intentions.

Finally, exhausted by the circular argument, they both step back and realize what's happening. They weren't arguing about what was said—they were arguing about what one person thought the other meant by what they said. Two completely different conversations, happening simultaneously.

The less you trust your reactive thinking about others, the more space opens for genuine connection.

The Birth of Empathy

When you realize you're reacting to thought rather than people, something beautiful happens:

You pause before lashing out because you recognize that your emotional reaction might not be telling you the truth about the situation.

You become more curious and less defensive because you're not so invested in proving your interpretation is correct.

You start to hear what's really being said beneath the surface noise because you're not so caught up in your own mental commentary.

That's when empathy naturally arises. Not as something you have to work at or practice, but as what's left when you're not tangled up in your own narrative about what's happening.

Presence isn't a relationship skill you develop—it's what emerges when you're not lost in thought about the other person.

This is how compassion enters even the most difficult moments. When you're not defending your story about someone's behavior, you have space to actually see them, to wonder what might be going on for them, to respond from wisdom rather than react from interpretation.

I experienced this shift dramatically with my teenage stepson during a particularly challenging period. He was going through typical teenage stuff—testing boundaries, being moody, sometimes responding to simple requests with attitude or resistance.

My initial reaction was often frustration or taking his behavior personally. I would think things like "He's being disrespectful" or "He doesn't appreciate what we do for him" or "He's deliberately trying to push my buttons."

But when I started to see that these thoughts were creating my experience of him, everything changed. Instead of reacting to my stories about his behavior, I could see a young person navigating the complex transition from childhood to adulthood, dealing with hormones and social pressures and the normal developmental need to establish independence.

The same behaviors that used to trigger frustration in me became opportunities for understanding and connection. Not because I became a better stepparent, but because I stopped mistaking my thoughts about his behavior for the truth about who he was.

The Freedom of Not Needing to Change Anyone

"You are never in love with anyone, you're only in love with your prejudiced and hopeful idea of that person." - Anthony De Mello.

One of the biggest relationship traps is trying to change others so we can feel okay. We think: "If only they would communicate differently, be more considerate, understand my needs better, then I could be happy."

But once you see that your emotional experience is internally generated—that it's coming from your thinking about them rather than from them directly—something radical happens:

You stop needing people to be different because you're no longer hostage to your interpretations of their behavior.

This doesn't mean becoming a doormat or tolerating genuinely harmful behavior. It means seeing clearly that your inner peace doesn't depend on outer compliance from others.

When you're not constantly trying to manage other people's behavior to protect your emotional state, you become much more effective at actually influencing positive change when it's needed. Paradoxically, when you stop needing people to change, they often naturally become more responsive and cooperative.

The Same Event, Different Movies

Let me give you some real-world examples of how this plays out:

Text Message: A simple "OK" response can feel warm and agreeable or cold and dismissive, depending entirely on your mood and the story you're telling yourself about the sender's state of mind.

Partner's Tone: The exact same slightly sarcastic comment can feel funny and playful or hurtful and mean, depending on your thought lens in the moment.

Child's Behavior: A tantrum isn't inherently a problem—it's your thoughts about control, failure, or disrespect that create your experience of it as problematic.

Coworker's Email: A brief, direct message can seem efficient and professional or rude and dismissive, based entirely on what you're thinking about the sender's intentions.

Same event. Different thinking. Completely different experience.

The Most Powerful Relationship Tool

Here's the most powerful relationship tool you'll ever have: the recognition that how you feel about others is never coming from them—it's always coming from your thoughts in the moment.

That's not a limitation. That's freedom.

Because while you can't control what other people say or do, you can remember where your experience is really coming from. And when you do, you stop reacting to illusions and start responding to reality.

You stop taking things personally because you see that your personal reaction is being created by your personal thinking, not by their impersonal behavior.

You stop trying to read minds because you realize that most of what you think you know about others' motivations and intentions is just mental storytelling.

You stop needing to be right about your interpretations because you see that they're just interpretations, not facts.

And in that space—the space that opens up when you're not defending your stories about others—real relationship becomes possible. Connection, understanding, love, and genuine communication can flourish when they're not competing with the noise of mental narratives.

Today's Simple Thought-Practice

This week, I invite you to experiment with this understanding. When you notice yourself having a strong emotional reaction to someone—whether it's irritation, hurt, anger, or even excessive admiration—pause and ask yourself:

"Am I reacting to this person, or am I reacting to my thoughts about this person?"

"What story am I telling myself about what their behavior means?"

"What if my interpretation isn't the only possible interpretation?"

You don't have to change your thoughts or try to think differently. Just notice that there's a difference between what happened and what you think it means.

That simple recognition—that moment of seeing the gap between event and interpretation—can transform not just how you feel in the moment, but how you show up in all your relationships.

Because when you're not busy defending your version of reality, you become available for something much more beautiful: actual connection with the real person in front of you, rather than your thoughts about them.

* * *

Key Insights:

- **You never react to people—only to your thinking about them.** Your emotions arise not from others' actions, but from the meaning your thoughts assign to those actions.
- **Your mind adds interpretation to every interaction.** A text, tone, or gesture is never experienced directly—it's filtered through personal thought, often without you realizing it.
- **The same person can feel totally different depending on your state of mind.** Because your perception changes with your thinking, so does your emotional experience of someone—even if they behave the same way.

- **Conflicts are rarely about facts—they're about clashing thought systems.** Most arguments are two people defending their separate interpretations, not disagreeing on objective reality.
- **Your experience of a relationship lives entirely in your own consciousness.** What feels like "relationship drama" is usually the byproduct of colliding narratives, not real interpersonal harm.
- **Seeing thought in the moment creates space for empathy.** When you pause and recognize your reaction as thought, it softens defensiveness and invites curiosity and compassion.
- **Presence happens when you drop the narrative.** You don't have to work at being present in relationships—just stop believing the stories your mind tells about others.
- **Empathy arises naturally when you stop reacting to your own mental commentary.** The more you see through your interpretations, the more clearly you see the humanity in others.
- **You don't need others to change in order to feel peace.** Once you realize your discomfort comes from thought, you stop needing people to behave a certain way to feel okay.
- **Not taking things personally becomes effortless.** You no longer need to manage others' behavior when you understand that your reactions come from within.
- **The same event can feel completely different based on your thinking.** A brief email, sarcastic joke, or child's tantrum isn't good or bad—it's your thoughts about it that define the experience.
- **Mental storytelling is the root of most relationship tension.** What creates conflict isn't what happened—it's the interpretation you're emotionally invested in.
- **You don't need to suppress emotions—just see where they come from.** There's no need to manage feelings or be less "reactive." Just notice that reactions are built from thought, not facts.
- **You can't read minds—most of your assumptions are fiction.** That imagined "tone" or "motive" is often just mental filling-in, not truth. Seeing this reduces unnecessary tension.

· **Recognizing the source of emotion is the most powerful relationship tool you have.** When you stop attributing your feelings to others, you reclaim your power and create room for real connection.

13

Trauma, Anxiety, and Depression - Why The Thought Principle Works In Big and Small Life Challenges

"You don't need to relive the past to heal. You just need to stop dragging it into the present with thought."

When people first hear about the Thought Principle, they often nod along with the everyday examples. They can see how their thinking creates their experience when it comes to work stress, relationship conflicts, or general life challenges.

But then they pause, and I can see the question forming in their minds before they even ask it:

"That's helpful for everyday stress... but what about the big stuff?"

"What about trauma?" "What about anxiety?" "What about depression?"

These are valid, important questions—and they deserve to be met with both compassion and clarity. Because here's what I've learned: the principles we've been exploring don't stop working when the pain gets intense. If anything, understanding them becomes even more crucial when we're dealing with the deepest forms of human suffering.

The Principles Don't Take a Break

The Three Principles aren't tools or techniques that you apply to certain problems. They're not a method for managing trauma, anxiety, or depression. They're the underlying explanation of how all human experience works—no matter how intense, no matter how overwhelming, no matter how real it feels.

That means:

Thought still creates experience, even when that experience is a panic attack.

Consciousness still brings thought to life, even when that thought is a traumatic memory.

Mind is still the source behind the system, even when the system feels completely broken.

This isn't about minimizing pain or suggesting that severe emotional distress is "just in your head." The experience is absolutely real. The suffering is genuine. The impact on your life can be devastating.

But understanding where that experience is actually coming from—and more importantly, understanding that it's not permanent—can be the difference between feeling trapped and finding freedom.

When the Volume Gets Turned Up

Here's something that took me years to understand: emotional intensity doesn't make something more true. It just makes it feel more true.

A panic attack feels absolutely real—your heart pounds, your palms sweat, your mind races with catastrophic thoughts. But it's still thought creating that experience. The thoughts might be louder, more urgent, more convincing than usual, but they're still just thoughts.

A depressive fog can feel eternal—like you've always felt this way and always will. But it's still thought creating that sense of hopelessness, that feeling of being trapped in a gray world where nothing matters. The thoughts might be heavier, more persistent, more all-encompassing, but they're still temporary mental events.

A traumatic memory can feel alive, as if the past event is happening right now. Your body might react as if you're in immediate danger, even though you're sitting safely in your living room. But that's thought bringing a memory to life in the present moment. The memory is real, the original event was real, but it's not happening now.

The louder the storm, the easier it is to forget that it's still weather.

This understanding didn't come easily to me. In fact, it took learning about Syd Banks' profound awakening to really see how these principles apply even in the most intense circumstances.

To refresh your memory from a previous chapter, Sydney Banks was a welder living on Salt Spring Island in British Columbia. He wasn't a spiritual teacher, wasn't particularly interested in psychology or philosophy. He was just an ordinary man dealing with ordinary problems—including what he later described as severe anxiety and insecurity that had plagued him for most of his adult life.

In 1973, at age 40, Sydney attended a weekend retreat with his wife. During one of the sessions, a psychologist made an offhand comment to him: "You're not really insecure, Syd. You just think you are."

Something about those words struck Sydney in a way that changed everything. In that moment, he had what he later called "an explosion of consciousness"—a profound realization that his entire experience of insecurity, anxiety, and personal suffering was being created by his own thinking.

He saw, with crystal clarity, that he wasn't an insecure person having insecure thoughts. He was a healthy, whole human being who had been innocently believing insecure thoughts and mistaking them for reality.

The transformation was immediate and permanent. The anxiety that had tormented him for decades simply disappeared—not because he had learned to manage it or cope with it, but because he saw through the illusion that had been creating it.

Sydney's story shows us that no matter how intense our suffering feels, no matter how long we've been trapped in patterns of anxiety, depression, or trauma, we are never more than one insight away from freedom.

The Myth of Necessary Suffering

One of the most liberating truths I've discovered is this: you can heal without revisiting the pain. You don't need to relive trauma to outgrow it. You don't need to analyze every aspect of your depression to move beyond it. You don't need to understand the root cause of your anxiety to find peace.

Why? Because trauma, depression, and anxiety are all memories or thought patterns experienced through present-moment thinking.

No. You can go. It's that simple.

When your thinking changes—when you see something new, when insight strikes, when understanding deepens—your experience of the past can shift instantly, without effort, without having to go back and "work through" anything.

This goes against everything we've been taught about healing. We've been told that we need to process our trauma, even go to battle with them, that we need to understand our patterns, that we need to do the hard work of excavating our past and making sense of it all.

But what if that's not true? What if healing is not about changing your past but about waking up to the fact that the past is not happening now?

That was the profound lesson I learned on that first day of that psychedelic retreat.

Consider the experience many people have with childhood bullying. Someone might carry the emotional scars of being tormented at school for years, even decades. They might avoid social situations, struggle with self-confidence, or find themselves constantly anticipating rejection or humiliation. The original events happened long ago, but they continue to shape their daily experience.

Traditional approaches might focus on processing those memories, understanding their impact, building coping strategies, or gradually exposing the person to similar situations to desensitize them.

But what if the real issue isn't the past events themselves, but the present-moment thoughts about those events? What if every time they feel that familiar anxiety in a social situation, they're not actually experiencing the original bullying—they're experiencing their current thinking about the possibility of being rejected or humiliated?

When someone sees this clearly—when they recognize that they're not reliving the past but creating a present-moment experience through their thinking—something profound can shift. The memories don't disappear, but they lose their emotional charge. They become just information about things that happened, no more significant than remembering what they had for lunch last Tuesday.

This isn't about denying the reality of what happened or minimizing its impact. It's about recognizing that the ongoing suffering is being created fresh in each moment through thought, not by the past events themselves.

Beyond the Labels

Here's something important to understand: a diagnosis is not a life sentence. It's a label describing a collection of thought patterns and felt experiences that tend to occur together.

Anxiety is not a personality trait—it's a temporary state created by anxious thinking.

Depression is not your identity—it's a fog that lifts when thought clears.

PTSD is real and can be debilitating—but it's still driven by thought reactivating past impressions in the present moment.

This doesn't mean that medication or therapy are wrong. For many people, these interventions can be helpful, even life-saving. But it does mean that you're not fundamentally broken. You're not damaged goods. You're not stuck with a faulty operating system.

You're just caught in a misunderstanding about where your experience is coming from.

You don't need to fix the machine. You just need to stop mistaking its noise for truth.

Think about someone who's been told they have "chronic anxiety." Maybe they've had panic attacks, maybe they worry constantly about their health, their relationships, their future. Over time, they start to see anxiety as part of their identity. "I'm an anxious person," they say. "I've always been this way."

The label becomes a lens through which they view everything. Every racing heart becomes evidence of their anxiety disorder. Every worried thought proves they're broken. Every moment of calm feels temporary, like they're just waiting for the other shoe to drop.

But what if anxiety isn't who they are? What if it's just a pattern of thinking they've gotten caught in? What if every anxious moment is actually a fresh creation, happening right now through their current thinking, rather than some permanent feature of their personality?

When someone begins to see anxiety as a temporary state rather than a fixed identity, something shifts. They stop feeding the anxious thoughts with so much attention and belief. They start to notice that anxiety comes and goes like weather, and that underneath it all, they're still the same whole, healthy person they've always been.

The anxiety might not disappear overnight, but it loses its grip. It becomes just another experience passing through, rather than the defining feature of who they are.

The Path of Grace

So what actually helps when you're dealing with intense emotional pain? How do you apply this understanding when you're in the middle of a panic attack or trapped in a depressive episode or triggered by a traumatic memory?

The way forward isn't effort—it's grace. It's gentleness. It's the kind of compassion you would show to a frightened child.

Don't judge the pain. It's there for a reason, even if that reason isn't immediately clear.

Don't identify with the story your mind is telling you about what the pain means. You are not your trauma, your anxiety, or your depression.

Don't fight the experience. Fighting creates more turbulence, more thought, more suffering.

Just remember: this too is thought. This too is temporary. This too will pass.

Let the system do what it does best: reset itself. Your only job is to stay curious and open to the possibility that things can shift, even when they feel impossibly stuck.

The Light Through the Cracks

If you've been living under the weight of past pain, caught in anxious cycles, or lost in the fog of depression, I want you to know this:

You are not damaged. You are not stuck. And you are never more than one insight away from freedom.

That insight might not come all at once. Healing rarely happens in a straight line. But even a crack in the wall is enough for the light to start pouring in.

Sometimes that crack comes in the form of a moment when you realize you're watching your thoughts rather than being consumed by them.

Sometimes it's the recognition that you've been carrying the past into the present through your thinking.

Sometimes it's simply the understanding that what you're experiencing, no matter how intense, is not permanent.

These moments of clarity might be brief at first. The old patterns might reassert themselves. But once you've seen through the illusion even once, you can never completely unsee it.

And each time you remember—each time you return to the understanding that you are not your thoughts, that your experience is created from the inside out, that peace is your natural state—it becomes a little easier to find your way back home.

The storm might still rage for a while. But you'll know, in your bones, that you are not the storm. You are the sky in which all weather passes.

And that knowing, that remembering, that simple recognition of who you really are—that's where healing lives.

* * *

Key Insights:

- **Healing doesn't require revisiting the past.** You don't have to relive trauma or dig through old wounds to heal—you only need to stop recreating them with your present thinking.
- **The Thought Principle applies even in extreme suffering.** No matter how intense an experience—panic, depression, or trauma—it's still created via thought brought to life in consciousness.
- **Emotional intensity doesn't make something more real.** Just because pain feels overwhelming doesn't mean it reflects truth—it reflects the vividness of your thinking in the moment.
- **Trauma is memory re-lived, not re-happening.** When the past feels alive, it's because thought has brought it into the now—not because the event is actually recurring.
- **We suffer in the present, not the past.** Ongoing pain is created in real-time through current thinking, not through the original experience itself.
- **Sydney Banks' insight reveals the path to healing.** He saw that he wasn't an insecure man, just someone believing insecure thoughts—his anxiety vanished not through effort, but through clarity.
- **You don't need to fix yourself—you were never broken.** Mental distress doesn't mean you're flawed. It means you're caught in the illusion that thought is truth.
- **Thought makes suffering feel permanent, but it isn't.** Depression, anxiety, and trauma feel endless because of persistent thinking, not because they define who you are.
- **Healing happens through insight, not analysis.** You don't need to dissect the past to find peace. A single shift in understanding can collapse the weight of a lifetime of pain.
- **Labels are descriptions, not destiny.** Conditions like PTSD or anxiety are patterns of thought, not fixed traits or life sentences.

- **Medication and therapy can help—but you're still whole.** While some interventions are useful, your wellness doesn't depend on them. You're never beyond your mind's innate capacity to reset.
- **You are not your diagnosis.** Being labeled anxious or depressed doesn't define you. These are temporary states, not permanent identities.
- **The less you believe your thoughts, the more freedom you find.**
- Anxious, depressive, or traumatic thinking loses its grip the moment you recognize it as thought—not truth.
- **Insight is the gateway to transformation.** You're never more than one realization away from peace—even if your journey has been long and hard.
- **The storm isn't you.** You are not your thoughts or feelings. You are the awareness in which all experience arises and passes. You are the sky, not the weather.

14

Thought & Spirituality – Seeing Through the Illusion of Form

"You are not the voice in your head. You are the awareness that hears it."

W hat if you've never been separate from peace? What if your problems aren't just in your head... but the self that you identify as is too?

That's not philosophy or spiritual theory. That's a pointer to something you can discover directly, right here, right now.

The deeper you see into the nature of thought, the more the illusion of the personal self begins to dissolve. And what's left when that happens isn't nothing—it's everything. It's the vast, spacious awareness that you've always been, temporarily obscured by the mental construction of a separate "me."

This might sound abstract or mystical, but it's actually the most practical understanding you could ever have. Because when you see through the illusion of the separate self, you stop trying to fix, improve, or protect something that was never real in the first place.

The Construction Project

It's relatively easy to see that worry is thought. Most people can recognize that anxiety, stress, and negative emotions are created by thinking. But here's what's harder to see—and infinitely more freeing—the "you" that experiences those emotions is also thought.

Your name, your backstory, your beliefs, your preferences, your person-ality traits, your strengths and weaknesses, even the voice narrating your experience right now—all of it is constructed in real-time through thought.

The "you" you think you are is a character inside a thought-dream, no more solid or permanent than a character in a nighttime dream.

This isn't theory or philosophy. You can feel this truth directly when the mind quiets, when thought settles, when you glimpse the space between thoughts. In those moments, there's awareness, but no sense of a separate "me" having the awareness. There's just... being.

I remember the first time I really saw this clearly. I was sitting in meditation—not trying to achieve anything, just sitting quietly—when sud-denly the sense of "Ray" completely disappeared. There was still awareness, still presence, but no one there to be aware or present. It was like the character in the movie had vanished, but the screen was still there, still displaying the movie.

For a few moments, there was no meditator, no one trying to be spiritual, no one with problems to solve or goals to achieve. Just pure, open awareness, completely at peace, completely whole.

When the sense of "me" returned—and it did, as it always does—I realized I had been living inside a case of mistaken identity. I had been thinking I was the character, when I was actually the screen on which all characters appear and disappear.

The Fog on the Mirror

Imagine a mirror covered in fog. That's what life looks like when thought is constantly streaming, when the mind is busy creating and maintaining the story of "me" and "my life" and "my problems."

Now imagine the fog clears—just a little. For a moment, you see not just the world more clearly, but yourself clearly. And what you see isn't who you thought you were.

You glimpse:

Stillness that doesn't depend on circumstances being still.

Spaciousness that contains all experience without being touched by any of it.

Awareness without a narrator commenting on what's being experienced.

Peace without cause, love without object, joy without reason.

This isn't the result of spiritual effort or years of practice. It's your natural state, revealed when thought drops away like fog lifting from a landscape that was always there.

Most spiritual seeking is based on the assumption that you need to get somewhere, become someone, or achieve some special state. But what if you're already what you're seeking? What if the peace you're looking for is what you are when you're not busy being someone else?

Waking Up from the Dream

Think of life like a nighttime dream. While you're dreaming, everything seems completely real. Emotions arise, events happen, other people interact with you, and you have a strong sense of "me" experiencing it all.

But the moment you wake up, you realize that none of it was actually you. You were the dreamer, not the dream character. The "you" in the dream was just a mental construction, a temporary identity created by the dreaming mind.

That's exactly what happens when you wake up from the illusion of thought. You don't become spiritual—you realize you are what spirituality has always been pointing to. You realize you don't have a soul, you are the soul.

You see that the "you" who has been seeking peace, trying to solve problems, working on self-improvement, and struggling with life is just a thought-created character. The real you—the awareness in which all experience arises—has never been touched by any of the drama.

This realization doesn't make you indifferent or disconnected. If anything, it makes you more present, more loving, more responsive to life. But you're no longer taking the personal drama so seriously because you see it for what it is—a temporary play of consciousness, no more real than a movie on a screen.

The Pathless Path

Here's the beautiful thing about this understanding: you don't need to do anything to realize it. You don't need to:

Meditate for hours to quiet your mind. Work on releasing your ego or transcending your personality. Fix your chakras, clear your energy, or purify your consciousness. Follow complex spiritual practices or study ancient texts. Or even fly to Jamaica to swallow a bunch of magic mushroom capsules.

You just need to see clearly that the ego—the sense of being a separate self with problems to solve and goals to achieve—isn't real. It's a loop of thought pretending to be you.

And the more often you see through this illusion, the less seriously you take it. You start to relate to your thoughts and emotions the way you might relate to characters in a movie—interesting, sometimes entertaining, occasionally dramatic, but not ultimately real or important.

The quiet behind thought isn't emptiness or void. It's presence, aliveness, the very essence of what you are. It's what's been here all along, patiently waiting for you to stop looking everywhere else for it.

I think about this every time I see a toddler play. They can be completely absorbed in an imaginary game, talking to invisible friends, creating elaborate stories with their toys. They're totally engaged, living fully in their make-believe world, but they never lose sight of the fact that it's play. They don't confuse themselves with the characters in their game or believe that the drama they're creating is ultimately real.

That's the kind of lightness that's possible when you see through the illusion of the separate self. You can still engage fully with life, have preferences, make decisions, care deeply about things. But you're not confused about who you really are underneath all the mental activity.

The Timeless Moment

What I want to point you toward isn't a future state you need to achieve or a special experience you need to have. It's what's here right now, in this moment, reading these words.

Notice that there's awareness of these words appearing in consciousness. Notice that this awareness doesn't have a name, an age, a history, or a story. It's just pure knowing, pure presence.

That awareness—not the thoughts about the awareness, not the story of who's having the awareness, but the awareness itself—that's what you are.

It's not personal. It doesn't belong to you. You are it.

And it's never been touched by any of the thoughts, emotions, experiences, or circumstances that have seemed to define your life. It's been here through every joy and every sorrow, every success and every failure, every moment of clarity and every period of confusion.

It's what remains when everything else falls away. And it's what you can rest in, right now, without needing to change anything about your life or yourself.

Today's Simple Thought-Practice - Seat of the Self

So if you've been searching for spiritual truth, if you've been trying to transcend your ego or find enlightenment, I want to offer you the simplest invitation:

You don't have to transcend thought. You just have to stop identifying with it.

You don't have to get rid of the ego. You just have to see that it was never real in the first place.

You don't have to become awakened. You just have to recognize that you've never been asleep—you've just been dreaming that you were someone else.

Imagine that you are sitting in a movie theater, watching a 90-year epic unfold on the screen before you. This film is filled with adventure and heartbreak, triumph and tragedy, love found and love lost. You witness the protagonist—who looks remarkably like you—navigate childhood wonder, teenage confusion, adult responsibilities, and all the joys and sorrows that make up a human life.

You watch this character face challenges that seem insurmountable, experience moments of pure bliss, struggle with difficult relationships, celebrate victories, mourn losses, and grow through every twist and turn of the plot. Sometimes the movie is a comedy, sometimes a drama, sometimes a thriller that has you on the edge of your seat.

But here's what's remarkable: no matter how intense the action becomes on screen, no matter how much the character suffers or celebrates, you—the one watching—remain completely safe in your seat. You are never actually hungry when the character goes without food, never truly in danger when they face peril, never actually heartbroken when they experience loss.

You might feel moved by the story, emotionally engaged with the character's journey, even brought to tears by particularly poignant scenes. But you never forget that you are the observer, not the observed. You are the awareness watching the movie, not the character in the movie.

That awareness—the one sitting safely in the theater seat, witnessing it all with compassion but never truly threatened by any of it—that is your true self. It is the part of you that has been present through every moment of your life, unchanged by any experience, untouched by any circumstance, constant through every season of joy and sorrow.

This awareness never ages, never hungers, never thirsts, never lives or dies in the way the character on screen does. It simply witnesses, loves, and remains—eternal, peaceful, and whole.

The movie of your life will continue to unfold with all its drama and beauty. But you are not the character struggling on screen. You are the timeless awareness in which the entire story appears and disappears, as real and as temporary as any movie you've ever watched.

What's underneath all the mental noise was never touched by fear, story, or suffering. Thought creates the illusion of form—including the form you call "me." But beneath thought is the timeless, spaceless awareness you've always been.

And it's always here, waiting—just one quiet moment away.

Not as something you need to achieve or earn, but as what you are when you stop trying to be anything else.

The dreamer was never lost in the dream. The dreamer was just temporarily fascinated by the story playing out on the screen of consciousness.

You are not the voice in your head. You are the awareness that hears it. You are not the character in the story. You are the space in which all stories unfold.

And that space—vast, peaceful, loving, and eternally present—is your true home.

Welcome back.

$$* * *$$

Key Insights:

- **You are not your thoughts—you're the awareness of them.** Your identity is not the voice narrating your experience, but the silent presence that notices it all.
- **The self is a mental construction.** The "you" you think you are—your name, past, preferences, problems—is built in real time through thought.
- **The personal self is an illusion.** What feels like "you" is just a bundle of habitual stories. When thought quiets, the separate self disappears.
- **Peace is not earned—it's uncovered.** True peace isn't something you work toward. It's what's left when the noise of thought drops away.
- **You are the screen, not the movie.** You aren't the character reacting to life's drama—you're the space in which the entire movie of life plays out.

- **Spiritual seeking reinforces the illusion.** Most spiritual practices subtly reinforce the idea that you're a self who needs to evolve. But there's nothing to become—only something to see through.
- **Stillness is your natural state.** Underneath all mental activity lies a vast, open, undisturbed awareness. It's not a goal—it's what you already are.
- **Waking up is seeing, not striving.** Enlightenment isn't something to attain. It's simply the clear recognition that you were never the character in the first place.
- **The ego is just a loop of thought.** What we call "ego" isn't a thing. It's a repetitive thought pattern pretending to be someone.
- **All drama is happening on a movie screen.** No matter how intense your experiences feel, they're like a film—you are never truly the one being hurt or praised.
- **Freedom comes from disidentifying with thought.** You don't need to control, heal, or transform your thoughts. You only need to stop mistaking them for who you are.
- **The true self is timeless awareness.** The real "you" doesn't age, fear, strive, or suffer. It simply watches, untouched, like the sky behind passing weather.
- **The present moment is always enough.** Right now, without adding anything, you can rest in what you are: pure presence, free from identity or story.
- **You are the dreamer, not the dream.** Your life may seem like a complex drama, but you are not the one struggling—you are the awareness in which it unfolds.
- **You're always one quiet moment away from home.** Returning to your true nature doesn't require effort—just a moment of not trying to be anything.

15

Thought & Performance – Why Clarity Outperforms Effort In Achievement

"You don't find flow by forcing it. You fall into it when thought lets go."

We're taught that peak performance comes from pushing harder. From hustling more, mastering every detail, staying hyper-focused, and controlling every possible outcome. The cultural narrative around success is built on effort, discipline, and the relentless pursuit of perfection through sheer force of will.

But here's the truth that elite performers across every field eventually discover: Your best performance doesn't come from trying harder—it comes from thinking less.

This isn't about being lazy or unprepared. It's about understanding that there's a fundamental difference between the effort required to develop skill and the state of mind that allows that skill to express itself most fully.

Let's explore why clarity—not effort—is the real secret to high performance.

The Disappearing Act

Ever been in "the zone"? That magical state where everything flows effort-lessly, where you're performing at your absolute best without feeling like you're trying at all?

Athletes call it flow. Artists call it inspiration. Public speakers call it presence. Musicians call it being in the groove.

But here's what's fascinating: what's missing in all those peak performance states?

Excess thought. The voice in your head analyzing every move. The "you" trying to do it right, worrying about the outcome, second-guessing every decision.

Flow is not a result of more thinking—it's the absence of unnecessary thinking.

When you're truly in the zone, there's no sense of effort, no mental commentary, no self-consciousness. There's just pure action arising from a quiet mind, like water flowing downhill or a bird in flight.

I remember watching a professional tennis player describe his experience during a particularly brilliant match. "I wasn't thinking about technique or strategy," he said. "I wasn't even thinking about winning. The ball would come toward me, and my body just knew what to do. It was like watching someone else play tennis through my eyes."

That's the paradox of peak performance: the better you perform, the less "you" there is doing the performing.

The Interference Pattern

When you choke on stage, freeze in an important meeting, bomb a big test, or blank during a crucial performance, it's not because you're weak or unprepared or fundamentally flawed.

It's because you're caught in too much thought.

Your mind gets loud—filled with worry about the outcome, analysis of what you should be doing, fear of what might go wrong, pressure to perform perfectly—and that mental noise drowns out your natural ability.

Think about it: you've probably given that presentation dozens of times in practice. You know the material inside and out. You've prepared thoroughly. But when it matters most, suddenly you can't access what you know.

What changed? Not your knowledge or your skill. What changed was the amount of thinking happening in your head.

When thought gets loud, clarity gets drowned out. And when clarity returns—often suddenly, without warning—your natural ability shines again. Not because you fixed yourself or found some new technique, but because you stopped interfering with what was already there.

I experienced this firsthand during a period when I was co-hosting a weekly radio program. I had developed a pattern of getting increasingly nervous before shows, to the point where I would sometimes lose my train of thought or stumble over words and topics I'd discussed hundreds of times before.

The more important the topic or the bigger the guest, the worse it got. I tried various techniques—breathing exercises, visualization, positive self-talk, over-preparing my notes—but nothing seemed to help consistently. If anything, the more I tried to manage my nervousness, the more nervous I became.

Then one day, I was running late for a show where I was hosting solo—always more nerve-wracking than having a co-host to lean on. I arrived at the studio just as we were due to go on air, barely having time to sit down and put on my headphones before the "on air" light came on.

I didn't have time for my usual pre-show anxiety ritual. No time to review my notes one more time, no time to do breathing exercises or give myself a pep talk. I just sat down and started talking.

It was one of the best shows I'd ever done. Fluid, natural, engaging. The conversation flowed effortlessly, insights arose spontaneously, and I felt completely present with both the material and the audience. Afterward, listeners called in to comment on how relaxed and confident I seemed, how authentic the discussion felt.

What was different? I hadn't had time to think myself into a state of nervous overthinking. I just showed up and trusted that I knew what I was doing—

which, of course, I did. All the preparation was still there, all the knowledge and experience, but it could finally express itself without interference from my anxious thinking.

The Power of Fresh Seeing

You can memorize a hundred strategies, study every technique, and practice until you're technically perfect. But one fresh insight in the moment will outperform all of that preparation.

When your mind is clear and quiet:

New ideas arise spontaneously, perfectly suited to the situation at hand.

Confidence feels natural because you're not questioning every move.

Creativity flows because you're not filtering everything through old patterns.

Action becomes effortless because you're responding to what's actually happening rather than what you think should be happening.

This is how jazz musicians can improvise together seamlessly, creating something beautiful that none of them planned. How athletes can make split-second decisions that turn out to be exactly right. How entrepreneurs can pivot in the moment and discover opportunities they never could have strategized their way to.

Insight lives in a quieter mind. When thought settles, wisdom emerges. When you stop trying to figure everything out, intelligence shows up.

The Art of Getting Out of Your Own Way

So how do you perform better? Paradoxically, by not trying to perform better.

Here's what actually improves performance:

Letting thought settle instead of stirring it up with analysis and worry.

Trusting the moment instead of trying to control every variable.

Listening to what wants to emerge instead of forcing predetermined outcomes.

Seeing thought as thought instead of believing every mental commentary.

You don't need more adrenaline, more pressure, more intensity. You need less interference.

Let your mind quiet, and let your natural wisdom and ability express themselves.

This doesn't mean being unprepared or careless. Preparation is important—it gives you the foundation of knowledge and skill that can emerge when the mind is clear. But there's a difference between preparing thoroughly and then trusting yourself, versus preparing thoroughly and then trying to mentally manage every aspect of your performance.

When the Mind Gets Quiet

Let me give you some real-world examples of how this plays out:

Athletic Performance: A basketball player "choking" at the free-throw line isn't experiencing muscle failure—they're experiencing thought overload. The same shot they've made thousands of times in practice becomes impossible when their mind is filled with pressure, expectations, and fear of failure.

Public Speaking: The fear that grips you before an important presentation isn't coming from the audience judging you—it's coming from imagined thought loops about what might go wrong, how you might embarrass yourself, or whether you're good enough.

Creative Work: Writer's block isn't a lack of talent or ideas—it's too much self-evaluation, too much thinking about whether what you're creating is good enough, original enough, meaningful enough.

Leadership Decisions: The paralysis that sometimes strikes in crucial moments isn't from lack of knowledge or experience—it's from overthinking all the possible consequences and trying to guarantee the perfect outcome.

Each one of these clears the moment you remember: it's just thought. The performance anxiety, the creative block, the decision paralysis—it's all created by thinking, not by the actual situation.

The Natural State of Excellence

Here's what I want you to understand: your best performances have never come from pressure, stress, or trying harder. They've always come from presence.

Think back to your own peak performance moments. Whether it was in sports, work, creative endeavors, or relationships—when were you truly at your best?

I'm willing to bet it was when you were fully present, when you forgot to be self-conscious, when you stopped trying to control the outcome and just responded naturally to what was happening.

That's not a coincidence. That's how the system is designed to work.

Your natural state is one of intelligence, creativity, and responsiveness. When thought settles, these qualities emerge effortlessly. When thought gets busy, they get obscured.

The Invitation to Trust

So if you want to be more creative, speak more powerfully, lead with greater impact, or perform at your highest level, here's my invitation:

Don't try harder. Think less. Trust more. Let clarity lead.

This might feel counterintuitive in a culture that glorifies hustle and effort. But the most successful people in any field eventually learn this secret: peak performance comes from a quiet mind, not a busy one.

To be clear, I'm not instructing you not to study, practice, and train hard. I'm saying that when it's time to perform, trust the preparation and just throw yourself into life and experience the experience without thinking of the outcome.

You already have everything you need. The intelligence, the creativity, the ability to respond perfectly to whatever situation arises—it's all already there, waiting to emerge when you stop interfering with it.

Your job isn't to create excellence. Your job is to get out of the way and let excellence express itself through you.

Because your best performance has never come from pressure—it's always come from presence. And presence is what you are when you're not busy being someone else.

Trust that. Let thought settle. And watch what wants to emerge when you stop trying so hard to make it happen.

The zone isn't a place you go to—it's what you are when you stop leaving.

* * *

Key Insights:

- **Peak performance comes from presence, not pressure.** Your best moments happen when you're not trying to perform—but simply responding naturally, without self-conscious effort.
- **Flow is the absence of unnecessary thought.** The zone isn't achieved by doing more—it shows up when the internal noise of thought quiets and you're simply in motion.
- **Excellence is your natural state.** You don't have to generate brilliance—it arises when interference drops away. You're designed for fluid, intelligent responsiveness.
- **Thinking less lets your wisdom shine.** When you're not analyzing or judging your performance in the moment, creativity, confidence, and clarity emerge naturally.
- **Overthinking is the true cause of choking.** You don't freeze because you're incapable—you freeze because thought gets loud and crowds out your innate ability.
- **Preparation is useful—but not in the moment.** Practice builds skill, but performance flows best when you let go of the plan and trust your preparation.
- **Insight outperforms technique.** A clear mind in the moment will always outperform over-rehearsed strategies. Fresh seeing beats scripted execution.

- **The harder you try, the tighter you grip.** Performance anxiety isn't a flaw—it's what happens when thought tries to control what should be intuitive and fluid.
- **The solution isn't managing thought—it's stepping aside.** Trying to fix your mindset just adds more thought. Real transformation happens when you stop interfering.
- **Trust is the gateway to flow.** When you trust that your system knows what to do, performance becomes effortless, alive, and free of pressure.
- **Creative blocks are mental traffic jams.** Writer's block, decision paralysis, and performance fear all stem from too much inner noise—not from a lack of capability.
- **The zone is what's left when the "you" disappears.** The best performances happen when the personal "me" doing the performing fades into the background.
- **You can't think your way into flow.** Flow isn't the result of cognitive effort—it's the absence of the egoic voice analyzing every move.
- **You already have everything you need.** Clarity, wisdom, and presence are not distant goals. They're already in you, revealed when thought lets go.
- **You don't need more effort—you need less interference.** Your job isn't to force excellence, but to get out of the way so it can emerge through you.

16

Creating Effortless Happiness & Joy With The Thought Principle

"True happiness isn't something you create—it's something you stop preventing."

Most people approach happiness like they're trying to fill a leaky bucket. They pour in achievements, experiences, relationships, and possessions, wondering why the good feelings keep draining away. They work harder, acquire more, optimize their lives with greater precision, all while missing the fundamental issue: they're trying to create something that's already there.

Understanding the Thought Principle reveals a radically different approach to happiness—one that's less about adding and more about subtracting, less about doing and more about undoing, less about becoming happy and more about recognizing the happiness that's been there all along.

The Happiness That's Always Here

Here's what I've discovered: happiness isn't an emotion you generate or a state you achieve. It's what remains when you stop interfering with your natural well-being through unnecessary thinking.

Think about the last time you felt genuinely happy for no particular reason. Maybe you were walking outside and suddenly felt light and free. Maybe you were doing something mundane like washing dishes when a sense of contentment washed over you. Maybe you woke up one morning just feeling good about life.

What was different about those moments? You weren't trying to be happy. You weren't working on your happiness or implementing happiness strategies. You were just... being. And in that simple being, without the mental effort to feel different than you felt, happiness was naturally present.

This is the happiness that the Thought Principle points toward—not the manufactured joy that comes from getting what you want, but the uncaused well-being that emerges when thought settles and you connect with your natural state.

```
"True happiness is uncaused."
```

The Happiness Thought That Causes Unhappiness

If happiness is natural, why don't we experience it more often? Because we unknowingly block it with certain types of thinking. Understanding these patterns can help you recognize when you're interfering with your own well-being.

The "When-Then" Trap "When I get the promotion, then I'll be happy." "When I find the right relationship, then I'll feel complete." "When I lose the weight, then I'll feel confident."

This type of thinking places your happiness in an imaginary future, making it conditional on circumstances aligning perfectly. But here's what actually happens: you get the promotion and feel good for a while, then your mind creates a new "when-then" scenario. The happiness you thought would come from the achievement was actually just the temporary relief from the thought that you needed it.

The suffering comes from believing that all the when-then statements are made of truth. In reality, they are just made of thought.

The Comparison Game

"She has a better job than me."

"They seem so much happier than I am."

"Everyone else has it figured out."

Comparison thinking automatically creates a sense of lack or inadequacy. But here's the thing: you're not comparing your actual life to their actual life—you're comparing your inside experience (which includes all your doubts and struggles) to their outside appearance (which you're interpreting through your own thinking).

The Problem-Solving Addiction

"I need to figure out why I'm not happier."

"There must be something wrong with me that I need to fix."

"If I could just solve this one issue, then I'd feel better."

This type of thinking treats happiness like a problem to be solved rather than a natural state to be experienced. The more you analyze your happiness (or lack thereof), the more you move away from the simple presence where happiness naturally resides.

The Perfectionism Prison

"My life needs to be perfect before I can be truly happy."

"I can't enjoy this because that other thing isn't right yet."

"Once I get everything organized/optimized/figured out, then I can relax."

Perfectionism thinking makes happiness conditional on an impossible standard. Since life is inherently imperfect and constantly changing, this approach guarantees that happiness will always be just out of reach.

The Natural Happiness Enhancers

Understanding the Thought Principle doesn't mean you become passive about happiness. Instead, you learn to work with your natural system rather than against it. Here are some ways to create conditions that allow your innate well-being to shine through more often:

Practice Thought Neutrality

Instead of trying to think positive thoughts, practice being neutral toward all thoughts. When you notice yourself caught in happiness-blocking thinking, you don't need to fight it or replace it with something better. Just recognize: "Oh, that's thinking," and let it pass through without giving it so much importance.

Embrace "Don't Know" Mind

One of the greatest sources of unhappiness is the belief that you should have everything figured out. But what if not knowing was perfectly fine? What if uncertainty was just another experience to be had rather than a problem to be solved?

When you can rest comfortably in not knowing—not knowing what will happen next, not knowing if you're making the right choices, not knowing how things will turn out—you free yourself from the mental strain of trying to control the uncontrollable.

Notice What You're Already Enjoying

Happiness often goes unnoticed because we're so focused on what's missing or what needs to be different. But right now, there are probably dozens of things you're enjoying that you're taking for granted: the ability to read these words, the comfort of wherever you're sitting, the fact that your heart is beating without any effort from you.

This isn't about forcing gratitude or positive thinking. It's about noticing what's already working, what's already pleasant, what's already fine exactly as it is.

Let Moods Move Through

Understanding the Thought Principle means recognizing that moods are like weather—they come and go naturally if you don't interfere with them. When you're in a low mood, instead of trying to think your way out of it or analyze why you feel that way, just let it be there. Low moods often precede insights or creative breakthroughs, and they always pass on their own.

Similarly, when you're in a good mood, you don't need to figure out how to maintain it or worry about when it will end. Just enjoy it while it's here, knowing that all moods are temporary.

The Paradox of Effortless Effort

Here's something beautiful about working with the Thought Principle: the less you try to be happy, the happier you tend to feel. This isn't because you're giving up on happiness, but because you're giving up on the mental effort that was blocking it.

It's like trying to fall asleep. The harder you try, the more elusive sleep becomes. But when you stop trying and just rest comfortably in bed, sleep comes naturally.

Happiness works the same way. When you stop efforting toward it and just rest comfortably in the present moment, it emerges on its own.

The Art of Allowing

Instead of trying to create happiness, practice allowing whatever is here to be here. If you're feeling frustrated, let yourself feel frustrated without making it wrong. If you're feeling peaceful, let yourself feel peaceful without trying to hold onto it. If you're feeling nothing in particular, let yourself feel nothing in particular.

This doesn't mean being passive about your life. It means being active from a place of ease rather than strain, responding to what's actually happening rather than what you think should be happening.

Following Your Natural Inclinations

When you're not caught up in should-thinking or trying to optimize every moment, you naturally gravitate toward activities and experiences that feel good. You might find yourself wanting to take a walk, call a friend, read a book, or just sit quietly. These natural inclinations often lead to more happiness than elaborate plans or forced activities.

The Ripple Effect

One of the most beautiful aspects of understanding happiness through the Thought Principle is how it affects others. When you're not desperately trying to be happy or constantly working on yourself, you become more present and available to the people around you.

You stop needing others to behave in certain ways for you to feel good. You stop taking their moods personally. You become a source of ease rather than tension, because you're not carrying the heavy energy of someone who's trying to fix their life.

This creates a positive ripple effect. People feel more relaxed around you because you're more relaxed within yourself. Relationships become easier because you're not looking to them to provide your happiness. Work becomes more enjoyable because you're not depending on it to fulfill you.

Why Stuff Never Makes You Happy, Even Though It Feels Like It Does

Here's the part that trips most people up: if happiness is already here, why does it feel so tied to getting what you want? Why does acquiring things seem to create genuine joy, even if it's temporary?

Let's walk through this carefully, because understanding this mechanism is crucial to experiencing more consistent well-being.

Picture this: You're driving along, feeling perfectly fine. Then a beautiful new car passes by—your dream car—and suddenly you're restless. A thought arises: "I need that car to be happy," and it feels completely true. Your contentment evaporates, replaced by a sense of lack and longing.

This is the first illusion: the belief that your happiness disappeared because you saw something you didn't have. But what actually happened? Your happiness didn't go anywhere—it got obscured by a thought about needing something else.

Eventually, you work hard and get the car. And for a brief, glorious moment, you feel elated, complete, satisfied. "See?" your mind says. "I told you this would make you happy!"

But look closely at what actually happened: the happiness didn't come from the car. It came from the brief silence in your mind when the wanting stopped.

The car didn't give you happiness—it just paused your desire. And in that pause, in that moment when thought settled and the mental chatter about needing something else went quiet, your true nature (which is naturally peaceful and content) briefly shone through.

It's like being in a noisy room and suddenly the noise stops. The silence was always there underneath the noise—you just couldn't hear it. The car didn't create your happiness any more than turning off a radio creates silence.

But then, just as predictably as sunrise, your mind grabs onto a new desire. Maybe now you need the premium sound system for the car. Or you start noticing other cars that are even nicer. Or you realize you need a bigger garage. The cycle continues, and your happiness once again feels dependent on getting the next thing.

Here's the key insight that the Thought Principle reveals: happiness doesn't come from getting what you want. It appears when the wanting stops—even for a second. It's revealed when thought settles, when the mental noise about needing to be somewhere else or have something else goes quiet.

This is why people can feel genuinely happy in the simplest moments—watching a sunset, playing with a pet, having a good conversation. In those moments, the wanting mind goes quiet, and your natural well-being emerges.

The Difference Between Attached and Detached Desire

This understanding leads to one of the most powerful distinctions you can learn, one that flows directly from seeing how the Thought Principle works:

Attached desire says: "I need this to be happy. My peace depends on getting this outcome. Without this, I'll be incomplete."

Detached desire says: "It would be wonderful to have this, but my happiness doesn't depend on it. I'm already okay, and this would just be a nice addition."

Attached desire is exhausting because it makes your well-being conditional on external circumstances that you can't fully control. You become a hostage to outcomes, constantly anxious about whether you'll get what you want and whether you'll be able to keep it once you have it.

Detached desire is freedom because it recognizes that your fundamental okayness doesn't depend on any particular outcome. You can still want things, work toward goals, and enjoy achievements, but your peace of mind isn't held hostage by whether you get them.

The difference isn't in what you want—it's in your relationship to the wanting. It's in seeing that the thoughts about needing something to be happy are just thoughts, not truths about your condition.

A Personal Example

I experienced this shift dramatically with my relationship to Apple products. I'm what you might call an "Apple junkie"—for years, I was completely caught up in their product cycle, believing that each new device would somehow enhance my life in meaningful ways.

Every time Apple announced a new iPhone, MacBook, or iPad, I'd watch the keynote presentation and feel that familiar surge of desire. The marketing was masterful: they'd show me exactly what was "wrong" with my current device and how the new one would solve problems I didn't even know I had. Suddenly, my perfectly functional phone felt outdated, slow, inadequate.

The thought would arise: "I need this new device. It will make me more productive, more creative, more connected." And that thought felt completely true. I'd convince myself it was a practical decision, a necessary upgrade for my work.

So I'd get the new device, and for a brief period, I'd feel genuinely satisfied. The unboxing experience, the sleek design, the new features—it all felt like progress, like I'd improved my life in some tangible way.

But then, as predictably as clockwork, Apple would announce the next version. And suddenly, my "latest and greatest" device felt old again. The cycle would repeat: desire, acquisition, brief satisfaction, then desire for the next thing.

What I began to see through understanding the Thought Principle was that my happiness wasn't actually coming from the devices themselves. It was coming from the temporary pause in wanting that occurred when I got what I thought I needed.

The new iPhone didn't make me happier—it just quieted the thought that I needed a new iPhone. And that mental quiet, that brief absence of wanting, allowed my natural contentment to emerge.

But Apple's genius is that they immediately create new thoughts about what you're missing. Before you can settle into satisfaction with what you have, they're already showing you what you don't have.

When I saw this pattern clearly, something shifted. I could still appreciate good design and useful technology, but I stopped believing that my well-being depended on having the latest version of anything. I realized I had been outsourcing my sense of progress and satisfaction to a product release cycle.

This doesn't mean I stopped buying Apple products entirely. It means I stopped being enslaved by the belief that I needed them to be happy or productive. Now when I see a new product announcement, I can appreciate the innovation without feeling that familiar tug of "I must have this."

The freedom isn't in rejecting technology—it's in seeing through the thought that any external thing holds the key to your contentment.

The Freedom of Seeing Through the Illusion

When you really understand this mechanism—how thought creates the illusion that happiness comes from external things—you start to relate to your desires differently. You can still enjoy nice things (I still buy Apple gadgets), pursue meaningful goals, and appreciate beautiful experiences. But you're no longer enslaved by the belief that your happiness depends on getting them.

This creates a beautiful paradox: the less you need things to make you happy, the more you can actually enjoy them when they show up. You're no longer grasping so tightly that you squeeze the joy out of everything.

You start to see that the happiness you've been chasing through achievements and acquisitions has been with you all along, just temporarily obscured by thoughts about needing to be somewhere else or have something more.

And in that recognition, you discover something remarkable: you already have everything you need to be happy. Not because your circumstances are perfect, but because happiness isn't dependent on circumstances in the first place.

The Daily Experience

So what does this look like in daily life? How do you actually live with this understanding?

Morning Awareness

Instead of immediately jumping into your to-do list or checking your phone, take a moment to notice how you feel when you first wake up. Often, there's a natural peace present before the mind gets busy with the day's concerns. You don't need to do anything with this awareness—just notice it.

Thought Watching

Throughout the day, occasionally check in with your thinking. Are you caught in happiness-blocking patterns? Are you making your well-being conditional on something changing? You don't need to fix anything—just notice.

Micro-Moments of Appreciation

Look for tiny moments of enjoyment that are already happening: the taste of your coffee, the feeling of sunlight on your skin, the sound of laughter from another room. These aren't things you need to create—they're things you can notice.

Evening Reflection

Before bed, instead of reviewing what went wrong or what you need to do tomorrow, notice what felt easy or pleasant about the day. What moments did you feel naturally content? What happened when you weren't trying so hard? How often did you catch yourself getting caught up in the illusion and bring yourself back to your True Nature?

The Ultimate Understanding

Here's what I want you to remember: you don't need to become someone who's good at being happy. You already are someone who's naturally happy— you've just been temporarily confused by thoughts that suggest otherwise.

The Thought Principle doesn't give you techniques for manufacturing happiness. It shows you how to stop manufacturing unhappiness. It reveals that beneath all the mental effort to feel different, beneath all the thinking, there's a well-being that was never actually disturbed.

Your job isn't to create this happiness—it's to stop preventing it. And you prevent it not through your circumstances or your past or your personality, but through believing thoughts that tell you happiness is somewhere else, in some other moment, dependent on some other condition.

The happiness you're looking for isn't in the future. It's not in the next achievement or the next relationship or the next anything. It's here, now, in this moment, available the instant you stop looking elsewhere for it.

And the most beautiful part? You don't have to take my word for it. You can discover this for yourself, right now, by simply noticing what's here when you're not trying to be anywhere else.

That's where happiness lives—not in the getting, but in the being. Not in the becoming, but in the recognizing. Not in the effort, but in the ease of simply being yourself, exactly as you are, in this moment.

Welcome to the happiness that was never missing.

* * *

Key Insights:

- **Happiness isn't achieved—it's revealed.** Your natural state is one of well-being, and happiness arises when thought interference subsides—not when conditions are finally right.
- **Trying to be happy often blocks happiness.** The mental effort to manufacture or chase happiness creates the very disturbance that prevents you from feeling it.
- **True happiness is uncaused.** It doesn't come from achievements or acquisitions—it surfaces when you stop believing you need something else to feel complete.
- **Thought creates the illusion of lack.** You don't lose happiness because of reality—you lose it when thought convinces you that something is missing.
- **The "when-then" trap postpones joy.** Tying happiness to future outcomes ensures you keep moving the goalpost and never arrive.
- **Comparison undermines inner peace.** Measuring yourself against others filters your lived experience through imagined stories that aren't grounded in reality.
- **The mind's attempt to fix happiness creates unrest.** Analyzing your happiness like a problem keeps you in your head and away from the presence where peace naturally lives.
- **Perfectionism makes happiness unreachable.** If everything must be ideal before you can feel good, you'll always find something lacking and

delay contentment.

- **Thought neutrality creates space for well-being.** You don't need to replace negative thoughts—just recognize them as thoughts and let them pass without assigning meaning.
- **Comfort with uncertainty dissolves inner pressure.** Letting go of the need to "figure it all out" invites peace to emerge in the space of not knowing.
- **Appreciation already surrounds you.** There are unnoticed sources of contentment everywhere—if you stop scanning for what's missing, you'll see what's here.
- **Moods are weather, not identity.** Low moods pass when left alone. Happiness returns naturally when you stop resisting what is.
- **Effortlessness is the path to joy.** Like sleep, happiness comes most easily when you stop trying so hard to reach it and allow it to arise on its own.
- **Allowing creates emotional spaciousness.** By letting emotions be what they are without control or suppression, you stop generating resistance—and happiness finds room to emerge.
- **Natural desires guide you toward joy.** When you're not driven by "shoulds," you organically move toward what nourishes you without needing to overthink it.
- **Happiness has a ripple effect.** When you're no longer chasing happiness, your presence becomes easier, more accepting—and others feel that freedom too.
- **Getting what you want brings quiet—not happiness.** Desire creates mental noise. What feels like joy from achievement is really just a pause in the inner craving.
- **Desire isn't the problem—attachment is.** Wanting is fine. But believing you need something to be whole makes you a hostage to outcomes.
- **The quiet behind thought is contentment.** Your well-being has never been absent—just masked by noise. When wanting stops, the silence reveals what was always there.
- **The freedom is in seeing through illusion.** When you see that no thing out there can make you happy, you stop outsourcing peace—and reclaim

it as your birthright.

- **Daily awareness reconnects you with joy.** Noticing your moods, appreciating small moments, and pausing for inner quiet are all ways to stay in touch with the happiness that's already here.
- **Happiness isn't personal development—it's the absence of interference.** You don't need to become a better version of yourself to be happy. You need to stop identifying with thoughts that say you aren't enough.
- **You are happiness, before thought says otherwise.** The peace you're seeking is your original nature—present in every moment when you stop looking elsewhere.

17

The Truth Test

"You don't need to believe your thoughts. You just need to see them clearly."

"How do I know which thoughts to believe?"

This might be the most common question I hear from people who are beginning to understand the Thought Principle. Once you realize that thoughts aren't facts and that believing every mental commentary creates unnecessary suffering, the natural next question is: "Okay, but surely some thoughts are true and worth believing, right? How do I tell the difference?"

It's a fair question, and one that reveals how deeply we've been conditioned to see thoughts as either true or false, good or bad, worth believing or worth rejecting. But what if the entire premise of the question is based on a misunderstanding?

What if the goal isn't to become a better judge of which thoughts to believe, but to develop a completely different relationship with thinking altogether?

The Belief Trap

Let me start with something that might surprise you: you don't actually need to believe any of your thoughts. Not the "positive" ones, not the "negative" ones, not even the ones that seem obviously true.

This doesn't mean becoming a skeptic who questions everything or someone who can't make decisions. It means recognizing that thoughts are just mental events—temporary visitors in the space of your awareness—and that your well-being doesn't depend on having the "right" thoughts or believing the "correct" ones.

Think about it this way: when you're watching a movie, you don't spend time trying to figure out which scenes to believe and which ones to dismiss. You simply watch the story unfold, sometimes getting caught up in the drama, sometimes remembering it's just a movie, but never confusing the characters on screen with reality.

Your thoughts work the same way. They're just mental movies playing in the theater of your consciousness. Some are dramas, some are comedies, some are horror films, some are documentaries that seem very factual. But they're all just movies.

The Futility of Thought Management

I spent years trying to be a good curator of my thoughts. I would analyze each one: "Is this thought helpful or harmful? Is it true or false? Should I believe it or challenge it?" I had elaborate systems for categorizing my thinking, techniques for replacing "bad" thoughts with "good" ones, and strategies for maintaining positive mental states.

It was exhausting. And more importantly, it didn't work.

Because here's what I discovered: the moment you make yourself the judge of your thoughts, you've already lost. You've entered into a relationship with thinking that assumes some thoughts are problems to be solved and others are solutions to be maintained. You've made your peace of mind dependent on having the right mental content.

158

But peace of mind doesn't come from having the right thoughts. It comes from not being at the mercy of any thoughts.

The Simple Truth Test

So if you don't need to believe your thoughts, how do you navigate life? How do you make decisions? How do you know what's real and what isn't?

Here's the simple truth test I've discovered: instead of asking "Is this thought true?" ask "Is believing this thought helpful right now?"

Not helpful in some abstract, philosophical sense, but practically helpful for responding wisely to whatever situation you're facing.

Let me give you some examples:

The Worry Thought

Your mind says: "What if something terrible happens to my family?"

Instead of trying to determine if this thought is "true" (which is impossible since it's about an imaginary future), ask: "Is believing this thought helpful right now?"

The answer is almost always no. Believing worry thoughts doesn't protect your family or prepare you for anything useful. It just creates anxiety in the present moment about something that isn't happening.

The Self-Critical Thought

Your mind says: "I'm not good enough for this job."

Instead of debating whether this is true or false, ask: "Is believing this thought helpful right now?"

If you're about to give a presentation, believing this thought will likely make you nervous and less effective. If you're genuinely underqualified for something, the helpful response isn't self-criticism but honest assessment and appropriate action.

The Judgment Thought

Your mind says: "That person is so annoying."

159

Rather than trying to determine if your judgment is accurate, ask: "Is believing this thought helpful right now?"

Believing judgmental thoughts about others usually just creates internal tension and makes interactions more difficult. Whether the person is actually annoying or not is less important than whether holding onto that judgment serves you.

The Wisdom Behind Thoughts

Here's something important to understand: I'm not suggesting you ignore all thoughts or become someone who never thinks. Thoughts often contain useful information. The key is learning to extract the wisdom without getting caught in the drama.

For example, if you have the thought "I should call my mother," there might be genuine wisdom there—maybe you haven't connected with her in a while and it would be meaningful to reach out. But you don't need to believe the thought in order to act on the wisdom. You can simply notice the impulse and choose whether to follow it.

Or if you have the thought "I'm not prepared for this meeting," there might be practical information there about needing to do more preparation. But you don't need to believe the story about being inadequate or unprofessional. You can just take the useful action without the mental drama.

The Three Categories of Thoughts

While I don't recommend spending a lot of time analyzing your thoughts, it can be helpful to recognize that most thinking falls into three basic categories:

Practical Thoughts

These are thoughts about immediate, concrete actions: "I need to pick up milk," "The meeting is at 3 PM," "I should call the dentist." These thoughts are usually straightforward and don't require much belief or disbelief—they're just information about what needs to be done.

Story Thoughts

These are thoughts that create narratives about yourself, others, or situations: "I'm the kind of person who always messes up," "She doesn't like me," "This is going to be a disaster." Story thoughts feel very real and important, but they're usually just mental fiction based on incomplete information and past conditioning.

Wisdom Thoughts

These are thoughts that arise from a deeper intelligence—insights, creative ideas, or knowing that seems to come from beyond your personal thinking. They often feel different from regular thoughts: quieter, clearer, more spacious. They don't demand to be believed; they simply offer themselves for consideration.

The key is learning to recognize the difference between these types of thinking, not so you can believe some and reject others, but so you can respond appropriately to each.

Living Without Belief

What does it actually look like to live without believing your thoughts? Does it mean becoming indecisive, passive, or disconnected from life?

In my experience, it's exactly the opposite. When you're not constantly caught up in mental stories about yourself and your circumstances, you become more present, more responsive, and more capable of wise action.

You make decisions based on what feels right in the moment rather than what your thinking tells you should feel right. You respond to people based on what you see in front of you rather than the stories you've created about them. You take action from clarity rather than from the compulsion of believed thoughts.

This doesn't mean you never plan for the future or learn from the past. It means you don't get lost in mental time travel. You can think about tomorrow without believing anxious thoughts about tomorrow. You can remember yesterday without believing guilty thoughts about yesterday.

The Practice of Non-Belief

So how do you actually practice this? How do you develop a different relationship with your thinking?

Notice the Difference Between Thoughts and Reality

Throughout the day, occasionally check in with yourself: "What am I thinking right now, and what is actually happening right now?" You'll often find that your thoughts are about some imaginary scenario while reality is much simpler and more peaceful.

Question the Urgency

When a thought feels very important or urgent, pause and ask: "Does this thought require immediate belief and action, or can I let it be here without doing anything about it?" Most thoughts that feel urgent are actually just loud, not important.

Practice the "So What?" Response

When you notice yourself getting caught up in a story thought, try responding with "So what?" Not in a dismissive way, but in a genuinely curious way. "So what if I'm not the smartest person in the room? So what if this doesn't work out perfectly? So what if they don't like me?"

Trust Your Natural Intelligence

Instead of trying to think your way through every decision, practice trusting the intelligence that operates below the level of thought. This is the same intelligence that beats your heart and heals your cuts. It knows what to do, even when your thinking mind is confused.

The Freedom of Not Knowing

One of the most liberating discoveries you can make is that you don't need to have everything figured out. You don't need to believe the right thoughts or have the correct opinions about everything. You can live comfortably in not knowing, responding to life as it unfolds rather than trying to control it through mental management.

This doesn't make you passive or irresponsible. If anything, it makes you more responsive because you're not filtering everything through layers of believed thoughts. You can see situations more clearly and respond more appropriately when you're not caught up in mental stories about what everything means.

The Ultimate Non-Belief

Here's the deepest level of this understanding: you don't even need to believe the thought that you shouldn't believe your thoughts. You don't need to believe anything I've written in this book. You don't need to believe in the Thought Principle or any other principle.

You just need to notice what happens when you hold your thoughts lightly versus when you grip them tightly. You just need to observe the difference between being caught in mental stories and being present to what's actually happening.

The truth will reveal itself through your direct experience, not through your beliefs about it.

So the answer to "How do I know which thoughts to believe?" is ultimately this: you don't need to know. You don't need to believe any of them. You just need to see them clearly, extract any practical wisdom they might contain, and let them pass through the space of your awareness like clouds passing through the sky.

In that space—the space that sees all thoughts but is captured by none—you'll find a peace and clarity that doesn't depend on having the right thoughts or believing the correct things. You'll discover that you are not your thoughts, and therefore you don't need to manage them, judge them, or believe them. You just need to be the awareness in which they all arise and pass away. And that awareness—that's who you really are.

* * *

Key Insights:

- **You don't need to believe any thoughts** - not positive, negative, or "obviously true" ones. Thoughts are temporary mental events, not facts.
- **The goal isn't better thought management** - it's developing a completely different relationship with thinking altogether.
- **Replace "Is this thought true?" with "Is believing this thought helpful right now?"** - Focus on practical usefulness, not abstract truth.
- **Three types of thoughts:** Practical (concrete actions), Story (narratives about self/others), and Wisdom (insights from deeper intelligence).
- **Worry thoughts are rarely helpful** - they create present-moment anxiety about imaginary futures without protecting or preparing you.
- **Living without belief makes you more responsive, not less** - you act from clarity rather than mental compulsion.
- **Notice the difference between thoughts and reality** - Often your thoughts are about imaginary scenarios while reality is peaceful.
- **Question mental urgency** - Most urgent-feeling thoughts are just loud, not actually important or requiring immediate action.
- **Practice curious "So what?" responses** - "So what if I'm not perfect? So what if this doesn't work out exactly as planned?"
- **Trust your natural intelligence** - The same intelligence that beats your heart knows what to do, often clearer than thinking.
- **You can live comfortably in not knowing** - Don't need everything figured out to respond wisely to life.
- **Extract wisdom without believing the drama** - Take useful information from thoughts without getting caught in mental stories.

- **You don't even need to believe this principle** – Just notice what happens when you hold thoughts lightly vs. tightly.
- **Truth reveals itself through direct experience** – Not through beliefs about it or mental analysis.
- **You are the awareness in which thoughts arise and pass away** – That awareness needs no thoughts to be complete or at peace.

18

You're Never More Than One Thought Away

"You are never stuck. You are never broken. You are never more than one thought away."

Y ou don't need a five-year plan to feel better. You don't need to heal everything from your past first. You don't need to conquer your mind, master your emotions, or complete some elaborate personal development program.

In fact, here's the most hopeful truth I know: You are never more than one thought away from a completely different experience.

Not one year. Not one month. Not even one day. One thought.

This isn't positive thinking or wishful optimism. This is how the system actually works. And understanding this can change everything about how you relate to difficult moments, challenging periods, and the inevitable ups and downs of being human.

The Instant Shift

Have you ever experienced this? You're angry about something—really steamed, maybe even furious—and then suddenly you're laughing. Maybe someone made a joke, or you remembered something funny, or you just saw the absurdity of the situation.

What happened? Did you work through your anger? Did you process it or analyze it or use some technique to manage it? No. A different thought arose, and with it came a completely different experience.

Or maybe you've been stressed about a problem, your mind spinning with worry and worst-case scenarios, when someone gives you a hug or you step outside for a walk, and suddenly you feel calm. The problem didn't get solved, but your experience of it shifted entirely.

Or perhaps you've felt hopeless about a situation—convinced there was no way forward, no solution, no light at the end of the tunnel—when one new idea, one fresh perspective, one different way of looking at things changed everything.

That's because your experience isn't based on the situation you're in. It's based on the thought passing through your mind in that moment.

When the thought changes—even slightly—so does your world.

A new thought can be as small as a breeze, but it can part the clouds and reveal the sun that was always there.

The Myth of the Long Climb

When we're feeling down, stuck, or overwhelmed, it's natural to think we need to work our way out gradually. We tell ourselves:

"I need to work through this." "I have to dig myself out step by step." "This is going to take time." "I need to process all of this before I can feel better."

But here's what I've learned: you don't climb out of thought with more thought. You don't think your way out of thinking.

The shift comes not from effort, but from insight. Not from analysis, but from a fresh seeing. Not from working harder on your mental state, but from recognizing that your mental state is just that—mental, temporary, changeable.

A single fresh thought can change your mood, your outlook, and your entire life trajectory. That's not an exaggeration—that's the miracle of being human.

That's exactly what happened to me during that psychedelic retreat in Jamaica. The medicine allowed my mind to go quiet in a way I had never experienced before, creating space for insight to shine through without the usual mental interference. For me, it came in the form of a divine presence and the profound words, "No. You can go. It's that simple," along with other revelations during the course of my journeys.

The insight was immediate and undeniable: all the suffering I thought was so real, so permanent, so much a part of who I was—it was all just thought. And thought, I suddenly understood with crystal clarity, could simply be released. There was no need to fight it, analyze it, or work through it. It could just... go.

Once the journey ended, I was different. Not because I had learned new techniques or developed better coping strategies, but because I had seen something fundamental about the nature of experience itself. I didn't have to work to maintain this new understanding—I just knew, somehow, that I was different. The shift had happened at a level deeper than thinking.

Over the coming months, when I was home and no longer under the influence of the medicine, insights continued to arise. Some would awaken me in the middle of the night, so clear and important that they beckoned me to write them down for safekeeping. It was as if my mind had been tuned to a different frequency, one where wisdom could flow more freely.

Then, on Thanksgiving morning at 5 AM, the accumulation of all these insights culminated in what can only be described as an "awakening experience." In that moment, I realized with stunning clarity that I'd been trying so hard to fix myself for years—decades, really—but in reality, there was nothing to fix. I had been whole all along, just temporarily confused about my true nature.

What struck me most was how effortless the whole transformation had been after that one pivotal insight. All the years of struggle, all the attempts to improve myself, all the searching for answers—and in the end, it was as simple as seeing through an illusion I had been carrying my entire life.

Your next thought could be the one that brings peace. It could be the one that shows you a solution you hadn't seen before. It could be the one that reminds you of who you really are underneath all the mental noise.

But here's the key: these insights can only flow freely when you're not gripping tightly to your current thoughts, when you're not magnifying them with endless analysis and mental elaboration. When you hold onto thoughts— turning them over and over, feeding them with attention, building stories around them—you create a kind of mental static that blocks the natural flow of fresh understanding. It's like trying to hear a whisper in a room full of shouting. The wisdom is always there, always available, but it needs space to emerge.

The Self-Correcting System

Here's something beautiful about how your mind works: you don't need to manufacture new thoughts. You don't need to force yourself to "think positively" or try to control what arises in your consciousness.

Your mind is designed to self-correct. It's like a river that naturally flows toward the sea, or a plant that naturally grows toward the light.

When you stop feeding the fire of stressful thinking, the flames go out on their own. When you stop resisting the storm of difficult emotions, it passes naturally. When you stop trying so hard to feel different, different feelings arise spontaneously.

And when this happens—when thought settles and clarity returns—it always feels like coming home. Not to a new place, but to where you've always been underneath all the mental activity.

That next helpful thought, that next insight, that next moment of clarity— it's already on its way. You don't have to earn it or work for it or prove you deserve it. It's part of the natural intelligence of the system.

Think about how this works in other areas of life. When you cut yourself, you don't have to consciously direct the healing process. Your body knows how to repair itself. When you're tired, you don't have to figure out how to sleep. Your system naturally moves toward rest.

The same is true for your mental and emotional well-being. There's an intelligence at work that's always moving you toward balance, toward clarity, toward peace. Sometimes we interfere with this process through our thinking, but we can never stop it entirely.

The Unbreakable Truth

No matter how long the fog has lasted, no matter how deep the spiral has gone, no matter how real the fear feels or how permanent the problem seems—you are never stuck.

You are never broken.

You are never more than one thought away from peace, freedom, or joy.

That thought might come today, or tomorrow, or in a quiet moment next week. It might arise while you're washing dishes, walking the dog, or having a conversation with a friend. It might come in the form of a memory, an insight, a sudden understanding, or just a simple shift in perspective.

But it will come—because insight is built into you. It's not something you have to create or achieve. It's something you are.

I think about all the times in my own life when I felt completely stuck, when I couldn't see any way forward, when I was convinced that my current state of mind was permanent. And I think about how, in every single case, something shifted. Not because I figured it out or worked hard enough, but because a new thought arose that showed me something I hadn't seen before.

Sometimes it was a big, dramatic insight that changed everything in an instant. Sometimes it was a small shift that gradually opened up new possibilities. But it always came, and it always came from a place I wasn't expecting.

That's the nature of fresh thinking—it's fresh. It doesn't come from your existing knowledge or your current perspective. It comes from the unknown, from the space of infinite possibility that's always available to you.

The Practice of Trust

So what's the practical application of this understanding? How do you live from the knowing that you're never more than one thought away from a different experience?

You trust the system. You trust that your mind knows how to reset itself, that your natural intelligence is always working on your behalf, that clarity is your default state even when it's temporarily obscured.

This doesn't mean being passive or giving up on taking action when action is needed. It means recognizing that your best actions, your wisest decisions, your most creative solutions come from a clear mind, not a busy one.

When you're feeling stuck or overwhelmed, instead of trying to think your way out, you can simply remember: this is temporary. This is just thought. And the next thought is already on its way.

You don't need to strive for it, reach for it, or make it happen. You just need to create space for it by not holding so tightly to the thoughts you're currently having.

The Infinite Possibility

Let this be your takeaway: You don't need to strive. You don't need to fix yourself. You don't need to control your mind or manage your emotions or solve all your problems before you can feel at peace.

Just understand the system. Understand that thought is temporary, that experience is fluid, that change is not only possible but inevitable.

And trust that the next thought is already on its way. It might be the thought that shows you a solution you hadn't considered. It might be the thought that reminds you of your own resilience. It might be the thought that helps you see the situation from a completely different angle.

Or it might simply be the thought that brings you back to the present moment, where you remember that you are not your thoughts, you are not your circumstances, and you are not your temporary emotional state.

You are the awareness in which all thoughts arise and pass away. You are

171

the space in which all experience occurs. You are the constant presence that remains unchanged while everything else flows and changes around you.

And from that place of knowing, every thought is a gift, every moment is a fresh start, and every experience is an opportunity to remember who you really are.

You are never stuck. You are never broken. You are never more than one thought away from coming home to yourself.

That's where all change begins—not in the future you're trying to create, but in the present moment you're already in, where the next thought is always, already on its way.

* * *

Key Insights:

- **A single thought can change everything.** You don't need a five-year plan or deep healing work. One new thought can instantly shift your entire experience.
- **Transformation doesn't require effort.** Change doesn't come from analyzing, fixing, or mastering your mind—it comes from seeing through the illusion of thought.
- **Your experience is thought in the moment.** It's never the situation—it's the thinking passing through you right now that creates what you feel.
- **Insight is faster than analysis.** Emotional shifts don't require processing—just a moment of fresh perspective that arises naturally when thought changes.
- **You don't climb out of thinking with more thinking.** Trying to manage your state with mental effort only keeps you stuck. Real change happens through insight, not strategy.
- **Peace is one insight away.** You're not far from clarity. It's often a single shift in perspective that parts the clouds and reveals your natural peace.

- **You are built for clarity.** Your mind is designed to reset itself. When you stop interfering, insight flows and balance returns on its own.
- **Healing is subtractive, not additive.** It's not about doing more—it's about letting go of the thoughts that obscure your inherent well-being.
- **The system is self-correcting.** Just as the body heals a cut, your psychological system self-adjusts when you stop fueling disturbed thought.
- **Struggle comes from clinging to thought.** You feel stuck not because you are, but because you're holding tightly to temporary thinking that feels permanent.
- **You don't need new tools—just new seeing.** Growth doesn't depend on more methods; it happens when you see through the illusion that you were ever broken.
- **Stillness invites wisdom.** When the mental noise settles, insight arises. Your next helpful thought comes from quiet, not effort.
- **Insight doesn't need conditions.** You might be washing dishes or walking the dog—and in that mundane moment, a thought can shift everything.
- **You've always been whole.** Every struggle you've experienced was built on a misunderstanding. When that illusion dissolves, your true self shines.
- **Awakening is a return, not a destination.** You don't become something new—you remember what was always there beneath the noise: presence, peace, and awareness.
- **The "stuck" feeling is a trick of thought.** No matter how real it feels, stuckness is just a temporary thought being taken seriously in the moment.
- **Fresh thought comes from beyond your current mind.** Your next insight won't come from what you already know. It comes from the unknown—from spacious, quiet mind.
- **You don't have to work for wisdom.** Just like sleep or healing, clarity arises naturally when you stop trying so hard to force it.
- **The mind is always moving toward balance.** You're wired for resilience and insight. No matter how deep the fog, your system is always guiding

you home.

- **You can trust the system.** Even when it seems like nothing is happening, insight is already on its way. You don't need to create it—just make space for it.

- **Peace is the default, not the prize.** Well-being isn't earned. It's what remains when you stop believing you're broken and trying to fix what was never broken.

- **You are not your thoughts.** You are the awareness beneath the swirl—the stable presence in which all thoughts and experiences come and go.

- **The present moment is your access point.** You don't need to wait for a better future. You're always just one thought away from remembering who you truly are.

19

Putting It All Together - The Art of Carrying Thought Lightly

"Freedom isn't the absence of thought. It's the absence of belief in every thought."

You've made it this far.

You've seen that you're not your thoughts—that you're the awareness in which thoughts arise and pass away. You've discovered that experience comes from the inside-out, that what you feel isn't created by your circumstances but by your thinking about your circumstances. You've understood that thought is temporary, not truth, and that insight—not effort—is what actually shifts everything.

So now what?

Now comes the beautiful part: you learn to live with thought. Not by managing it, controlling it, or trying to perfect it, but by carrying it lightly.

This is where the rubber meets the road, where understanding becomes a way of being, where you stop being a student of these principles and start being someone who embodies them naturally.

The Ongoing Dance

Let's get something straight right from the start: you're not going to "stop thinking." You're not supposed to. That's not the goal, and it's not even desirable.

Thought will keep showing up. Every day, probably every hour, maybe every few minutes. You'll still have insecure thoughts that make you question your worth. Judgmental thoughts that criticize yourself and others. Scary thoughts about the future, weird thoughts that seem to come from nowhere, irrational thoughts that don't make logical sense.

And that's perfectly fine.

Thought is not the enemy. It never was. Clinging to thought, believing every thought, taking every thought personally—that's where the suffering lives.

Think of thoughts like weather. You don't get angry at clouds for existing. You don't try to negotiate with rain or argue with wind. Weather just is— sometimes pleasant, sometimes challenging, sometimes beautiful, always changing.

Your thoughts are the same. They're just mental weather patterns moving through the sky of your consciousness.

The Shift in Relationship

What changes as you integrate this understanding isn't the presence of thought—it's your relationship to it.

You stop treating thoughts like facts that need to be verified or challenged.

You stop obeying every mental impulse as if it were a command from headquarters.

You stop reacting to every inner drama as if it were breaking news that requires immediate attention.

Instead, you get curious. You develop what I like to call "loving detach-ment"—the ability to observe your own mental activity with the same gentle interest you might have watching clouds form and dissolve in the sky.

"Oh look... thought is doing that thing again."

"Ah, here comes another storm. I wonder how long this one will last."

"That's a spicy thought—but I don't have to follow it down the rabbit hole."

This is how peace begins to become your default state, not something you have to work for or earn or achieve. It's already there, underneath all the mental weather, waiting to be noticed.

I remember a time I really experienced this shift. I was having one of those days where my mind was particularly active—jumping from worry about a work project to self-criticism about something I'd said in a meeting to anxiety about a family situation. In the past, I would have either fought with these thoughts or gotten completely swept away by them.

But this time, something was different. I found myself watching the whole mental parade with a kind of amused detachment, like someone observing a soap opera. "Oh, there's the work worry. And now here comes the self-criticism. And look, anxiety is making its entrance right on cue."

The thoughts were still there, but they felt... lighter. Less solid. Less important. Like background music in a restaurant—present but not demanding my full attention.

The River and the Dam

Here's a paradox that took me years to understand: the more seriously you take thought, the heavier it feels. The more lightly you carry it, the more freedom you experience.

It's like the difference between a river flowing freely and a river blocked by a dam. When thoughts flow naturally through your consciousness—acknowledged but not grasped, noticed but not clung to—they move like water finding its way to the sea. But when you build mental dams around certain thoughts, holding them in place, analyzing them, feeding them with attention and belief, they back up and create pressure.

Most people have built elaborate dam systems in their minds. Every worry gets trapped and examined. Every fear gets held and magnified. Every self-critical thought gets captured and replayed. The natural flow of consciousness becomes a series of stagnant pools, each one growing heavier and more overwhelming.

But when you learn to let thoughts flow lightly through your awareness, something beautiful happens. You can let thoughts pass through without being swept away by them. You can let moods rise and fall without taking them personally. You can let the inner commentary chatter away in the background without feeling compelled to believe every word.

You don't resist the thoughts—resistance just creates more turbulence. You don't chase after the pleasant ones—chasing creates attachment. You don't try to fix or improve or optimize anything.

You just let the river flow.

Beyond Technique

Here's something that might surprise you: once you really understand how thought works, you don't need techniques anymore.

You don't need thought logs to track your mental patterns.

You don't need cognitive reframes to change negative thoughts into positive ones.

You don't need mindfulness techniques to stay present.

You don't need positive affirmations to boost your self-esteem.

When you understand thought, the system self-corrects naturally. It's like learning how dreams work—once you understand that the monster chasing you in a nightmare isn't real, you stop being afraid of it. Not by fighting the monster or trying to turn it into something nice, but by waking up to the nature of the dream itself.

That's what living lightly with thought really is: waking up to the game of thought and choosing not to play so seriously.

This doesn't mean you become indifferent or disconnected. If anything, you become more present, more responsive, more alive. But you stop mistaking the mental commentary for reality. You stop believing that every thought deserves your attention or that every feeling needs to be analyzed.

What Integration Actually Looks Like

So what does this look like in real life? How do you know when you're actually living with thought lightly rather than just understanding it intellectually?

Here are some signs I've noticed in my own life and in others who've integrated this understanding:

You stop spiraling when moods dip. Instead of fighting low moods or trying to think your way out of them, you ride them like waves, knowing they'll naturally crest and fall.

You have more access to your wisdom, even in stressful situations. Because you're not caught up in the mental drama, you can hear the quieter voice of insight and intuition.

You feel more grounded, more present, more free. There's less mental noise competing for your attention, so you can actually be where you are.

You remember that none of it is personal. Thoughts arise from consciousness itself, not from some broken or flawed part of you that needs fixing.

You watch life like an interesting adventure movie, you understand that the challenges that always occur are what make life so damn interesting.

You'll still have ups and downs—that's part of being human. But you'll stop trying to build your identity around them. You'll stop needing every moment to be perfect, and instead, you'll let life flow.

I experienced this shift most clearly during a period when my business was going through some major challenges. In the past, this kind of situation would have sent me into weeks of anxious thinking, sleepless nights, and obsessive problem-solving.

But this time, while I certainly felt the stress and took appropriate action to address the issues, I didn't get lost in the mental storm. I could feel the worried thoughts arising, acknowledge them, and then return to a place of clarity where I could actually think strategically rather than reactively.

It wasn't that I didn't care or that I was in denial about the seriousness of the situation. I was just no longer confusing my thoughts about the situation with the situation itself.

Living Like Weather

So here's my final invitation to you: live with thought the way you live with weather.

Let it come. Let it go. Bring an umbrella when needed, but don't try to control the sky.

You don't need to master your mind. You don't need to achieve some perfect state of consciousness or eliminate all negative thinking. You just need to see through the illusion that your thoughts are more solid and permanent than they actually are.

When you do this—when you really get it, not just intellectually but in your bones—you'll start to feel what's always been there underneath all the mental activity: peace, presence, the simple joy of being alive.

This peace isn't something you create or achieve. It's something you uncover by removing the layers of mental noise that have been covering it up.

It's like discovering that the sun is always shining, even when clouds block your view of it. The clouds are temporary. The sun is constant.

Your thoughts are the clouds. Your essential nature—that aware, peaceful presence that you truly are—is the sun.

The Ongoing Journey

I want to be clear about something: this isn't a destination you arrive at once and then you're done. It's an ongoing dance, a continuous deepening, a way of being that becomes more natural over time.

You'll still get caught up in thought sometimes. You'll still have days when you forget everything you've learned and find yourself wrestling with your mind like you used to. That's not failure—that's being human.

The difference is that now you have a way back. You know that the storm is temporary, that clarity is your natural state, that peace is always available underneath whatever mental weather is passing through.

And each time you remember, each time you return to this lighter way of being, it becomes a little more familiar, a little more natural, a little more like home.

The Simple Truth

In the end, it all comes down to this simple truth: you are not your thoughts. You are the space in which thoughts arise and pass away. You are the awareness that remains constant while everything else changes.

When you really see this, when you really feel it, everything becomes lighter. Not because your life becomes perfect or your challenges disappear, but because you stop carrying the weight of believing every story your mind tells you.

You start to live with the freedom that comes from knowing who you really are—not the character in the story, but the awareness in which all stories unfold.

And from that place of knowing, life becomes an adventure rather than a problem to be solved, a dance rather than a battle, a gift rather than a burden.

That's the art of carrying thought lightly. That's the freedom that's always been available to you.

Welcome home.

* * *

Key Insights:

- **Freedom doesn't mean no thought—it means not believing every thought.** The goal isn't to eliminate thinking, but to stop taking every thought so seriously or personally.
- **Thought is not the enemy.** It's natural and ever-changing, like weather. Suffering comes not from thought itself, but from clinging to it.
- **The mind doesn't need to be managed.** You don't have to control, fix, or optimize your thinking. You just have to see that it's not always true.

- **Peace comes from relationship, not control.** You don't need fewer thoughts—you need a lighter relationship with the ones you have.
- **Let thought be weather.** Clouds pass, storms come and go. Let thoughts move through without gripping, resisting, or worshipping them.
- **Your relationship to thought is what changes.** The same thoughts may still show up—but now you see them for what they are: just passing mental activity.
- **Carry thought with loving detachment.** Instead of reacting, you can notice thoughts with gentle curiosity and let them go without drama.
- **The more seriously you take thought, the heavier it feels.** Lightness comes when you stop analyzing, clinging, or fearing every mental storm.
- **Trying to stop thought is resistance in disguise.** Don't fight your thinking—just stop fueling it with belief or attention.
- **Insight makes techniques obsolete.** When you deeply understand thought's nature, you no longer need affirmations, reframes, or mindfulness hacks.
- **You're not fixing thought—you're waking up from it.** Freedom doesn't come from managing thought, but from realizing it's not reality.
- **You're already peaceful underneath the noise.** Peace isn't something you gain; it's what's revealed when the mental clouds part.
- **You stop spiraling when you stop believing the spiral.** Low moods don't pull you under when you know they're temporary thought, not permanent truth.
- **You're not your moods.** Thoughts create feelings, but neither define you—they're just passing phenomena.
- **You're not broken, and never have been.** What felt broken was a misunderstanding—believing your thoughts too much for too long.
- **Let the river of thought flow.** The healthiest mind isn't a dam—it's a free-flowing river that doesn't hold on to every thought.
- **Real presence is effortless.** When you're not battling thought, you show up naturally—more aware, more intuitive, more alive.
- **You stop needing life to be perfect.** With less thought-gripping, you accept life's ups and downs without needing to be rescued from them.

- **Wisdom becomes audible when noise dies down.** Your deeper intelligence surfaces not from effort, but from space.
- **You see challenges as part of the story—not the whole story.** Life's obstacles become plot points, not evidence that something is wrong with you.
- **This is not a finish line—it's a practice.** You'll forget and remember again. Each time you remember, it becomes easier to return.
- **Peace is always there, even if thought blocks it.** Like the sun behind clouds, your natural well-being is never absent—just temporarily hidden.
- **You are the sky, not the storm.** Thoughts pass. Awareness remains. That's who you really are.
- **Welcome home—to what you've always been.** Freedom isn't something you chase. It's what you uncover when you stop following every thought.

About The Author

Ray Hinish is an entrepreneur, wellness practitioner, and student of human consciousness who discovered that the peace he'd been seeking through decades of personal development was available in a single moment of understanding.

For over twenty-five years, Ray has dedicated his life to helping people live healthier, longer lives through his wellness practice and radio show in Baltimore, Maryland. During that time, he helped tens of thousands of men and women transform their physical health—but he noticed something both peculiar and heartbreaking: people would learn the secrets of health and longevity, then return to lives filled with stress, anxiety, and quiet desperation.

Despite having healthier bodies, they were still struggling with restless minds.

This observation led Ray on his own journey of seeking, reading hundreds of books on psychology and personal development, attending countless seminars, and trying every technique promising inner peace. Yet for all his knowledge, he remained caught in the same mental struggles that plagued his clients.

Everything changed during a psychedelic retreat in Jamaica, where Ray experienced a profound awakening that dissolved decades of insecurity and self-doubt in an instant. In that moment, he heard a divine voice whisper, "No. You can go. It's that simple"—and suddenly understood that all his suffering had been created by believing his thoughts to be true.

This revelation transformed not only Ray's life but his approach to helping others. He realized that living a few more years is meaningless unless that life has meaning, peace, and genuine fulfillment.

Today, Ray continues to operate his wellness center in Baltimore, Maryland while sharing the understanding that changed his life. Drawing from the profound insights of Sydney Banks and the Three Principles, combined with his decades of experience in health, wellness, and coaching Ray helps people discover that they don't need to fix themselves—they just need to remember who they really are.

Ray lives with his wife and family, grateful for the simple recognition that transformed everything: you're not broken, you're just thinking.

If this book changed your life in any way, I'd love to hear from you.

Ray can be reached at ray@oneinsightawaybook.com

OneInsightAwayBook.com

www.ingramcontent.com/pod-product-compliance
Lightning Source LLC
LaVergne TN
LVHW051308080426
835509LV00020B/3160